广州铁路职业技术学院资助出版
校企合作双元开发活页式新形态一体化教材
高等职业教育铁道运输类"十四五"技能型人才培养实用教材

EMU Structure and Maintenance

动车组结构与维修（活页式）

主编 ◎ 南 松　滕世平

西南交通大学出版社
·成 都·

内容简介

本书为广州铁路职业技术学院与海外联合办学所使用的教材，适合双语教学。本书主要内容包括动车组机械设备的组成、结构、工作原理及维护与检修，图文并茂、通俗易懂。本书内容侧重基础，同时配以数字化的教学资源，以提高学生的整体认识，使学生初步了解动车组的一些基本概念和动车组一级修的内容。本书主要适用于动车组检修技术专业留学生作专业教材。

Brief

This book is a textbook for Guangzhou Railway Polytechnic and overseas joint education, which is suitable for bilingual teaching. This book presents the knowledge of the composition, structure, working principle and maintenance of the mechanical equipment of the EMUs, which is easy to understand, with pictures and texts. The content focuses on the basic knowledge and at the same time, it is attached with digital teaching resources to improve students' comprehensive understanding, so that students can have a preliminary understanding of some basic concepts of EMUs and the content of first-level repairs of EMUs. This book is mainly used as a professional textbook for international students majoring in EMUs maintenance technology, and can also be used as a popular science book for popularizing Chinese railway knowledge.

图书在版编目（CIP）数据

动车组结构与维修：活页式＝EMU structure and maintenance：英文／南松，滕世平主编. —成都：西南交通大学出版社，2023.1

校企合作双元开发活页式新形态一体化教材　高等职业教育铁道运输类"十四五"技能型人才培养实用教材

ISBN 978-7-5643-9150-8

Ⅰ.①动⋯ Ⅱ.①南⋯ ②滕⋯ Ⅲ.①动车－车体结构－高等职业教育－教材－英文②动车－维修－高等职业教育－教材－英文 Ⅳ.①U266

中国版本图书馆 CIP 数据核字（2022）第 256970 号

EMU Structure and Maintenance

动车组结构与维修（活页式）

主　编　南　松　滕世平

责任编辑	张文越
封面设计	何东琳设计工作室
出版发行	西南交通大学出版社 （四川省成都市金牛区二环路北一段 111 号 西南交通大学创新大厦 21 楼）
邮政编码	610031
发行部电话	028-87600564　028-87600533
网址	http://www.xnjdcbs.com
印刷	四川玖艺呈现印刷有限公司
成品尺寸	185 mm×260 mm
印张	9.25
字数	257 千
版次	2023 年 1 月第 1 版
印次	2023 年 1 月第 1 次
定价	42.00 元
书号	ISBN 978-7-5643-9150-8

课件咨询电话：028-81435775
图书如有印装质量问题　本社负责退换
版权所有　盗版必究　举报电话：028-87600562

前　言

随着中国高铁走出去的战略，中国铁路在东南亚各国取得了丰硕成果。在高铁装备走出去的同时，中国铁路的技术标准、管理标准等都将全面走出去。轨道交通维护与检修专业人才需求量越来越大，在轨道交通教育同步走出去的同时，轨道交通人才本地化也显得越来越重要。广州铁路职业技术学院主动对接国家"一带一路"倡议，与马来西亚拉曼大学学院开展合作办学，共同培养能从事动车组列车检修的一线岗位技术技能人才。

本教材根据动车组机械结构检修课程标准，并参考《铁路技术管理规程》《铁路动车组运用维修规则》《铁路动车组设备设计规范》等国铁集团规章和文件编写而成。

"动车组机械结构检修"是动车组检修技术专业的一门专业核心课，也是广州铁路职业技术学院招收马来西亚拉曼大学学院留学生必修课程之一，目的是让学生认识动车组的整体机械结构组成，使学生掌握动车组的车体、转向架、车体连接装置、基础制动装置等检修技能，具备动车组机械师的检修作业能力。

本教材实行以"项目导向、任务驱动、理实一体化"的教学模式，内容以动车组的构造和动车组的检修为主线，按照动车组的认识、动车组检修认识、动车组车体结构与检修、动车组转向架结构与检修、动车组车端连接装置结构与检修五个项目分层介绍，每一个项目都配有带有中英双语字幕的教学微课数字化资源，检修内容配有在动车组车间拍摄的实操演示视频，以最真实的一线车间工作任务展示动车组结构检修的过程，使学生直观了解动车组检修的全过程，培养学生遵章守纪、规范操作的职业意识。

本教材由广州铁路职业技术学院南松、滕世平主编，中国铁路广州局集团有限公司广州动车组段牛刚副主编，中车唐山机车车辆有限公司李会杰，广州铁路职业技术学院刘志运、马冬、颜秀珍，中国铁路武汉铁路局襄阳机务段将帅参编。

本教材在编写过程中参考了许多相关资料，谨向这些资料的作者致以最诚挚的谢意。

由于编者水平有限，书中难免存在不足之处，敬请广大读者提出宝贵意见和建议，以便在修订时改进。

编　者
2022 年 9 月广州

PREFACE

With China high speed railway export strategy, China railway has achieved fruitful results in Southeast Asian countries. While the high speed railway equipment is being exported, the technical standards and management standards of China railways will be fully promoted overseas. The demand for railway maintenance technicians is increasing. While railway education is overseas, the localization of railway personnel training is becoming more and more important. Guangzhou Railway Polytechnic takes the initiative to connect with the national "The Belt and Road initiative" and cooperates with the UTAR Malaysia in running schools to jointly cultivate technical and skilled personnel who can be engaged in the maintenance of EMUs.

This book is compiled according to the course standards for the EMUs mechanical structure, and with reference to the "Technical Management Rules of Railway""Rules for Operation and Maintenance of EMUs" "Railway EMUs Equipment Design Specification" and other regulations and documents of China State Railway Group Co., Ltd.

"EMUs mechanical structure maintenance" is a professional core course for EMUs maintenance technology major and it is also one of the compulsory courses for Guangzhou Railway Polytechnic to recruit international students from UTAR Malaysia. The aim is to let the students grasp the overall mechanical structure of the EMUs, so that the students can master the maintenance skills of the EMUs body, bogie, end connection device, foundation braking device, etc., and have the maintenance operation ability of the EMUs mechanic.

This book implements the teaching mode of "project-oriented, task-driven, theory and practice integration". The content is based on the structure of the EMUs and the maintenance of the EMUs. According to recognizing EMUs, EMUs maintenance, EMUs body structure and maintenance, EMUs bogie structure and maintenance, EMUs end connection device structure and maintenance, the five projects are introduced. Each project is equipped with digital resources for teaching microlecture with Chinese and English subtitles. The maintenance content is equipped with a practical demonstration video shot in the EMUs workshop, showing the process of EMUs structural maintenance with the most real front-line workshop tasks, so that students can intuitively recognize the whole process of EMUs maintenance, and train students to abide by the rules and regulations and operate in a standardized way. professional awareness.

This book chief editors are Nan Song and Teng Shiping of Guangzhou Railway Polytechnic, associate editor is Niu Gang of Guangzhou EMU Depot of China Railway Guangzhou Group Co., Ltd., Li Huijie of CRRC Tangshan Co., Ltd, Liu Zhiyun, Ma Dong and Yan Xiuzhen of Guangzhou Railway Polytechnic, and Xiangyang Locomotive Depot of Wuhan Group Co., Ltd., participated in the edit.

Many relevant materials have been referenced in the preparation of this book, and I would like to express my sincerest gratitude to the authors of these materials.

Due to the limitation of knowledge, there are inevitably shortcomings in the book. Readers are expected to provide valuable comments and suggestions for improvement during revision.

Authors
2022.9 Guangzhou

CONTENTS

Chapter 1　Recognizing EMUs ··· 001

   1.1　High-Speed Trains Around the World ································· 001
   1.2　Types of EMUs ··· 025
   1.3　EMUs Numbering Rules in China ··· 029
   1.4　Components of EMUs ·· 032

Chapter 2　EMUs Maintenance ·· 040

   2.1　EMUs Maintenance Procedures and Systems ······················· 040
   2.2　EMUs Maintenance Site ··· 045
   2.3　EMUs Maintenance Tools ··· 050

Chapter 3　EMUs Body Structure and Maintenance ······················ 062

   3.1　EMUs Body Structure ·· 062
   3.2　EMUs Body Composition ·· 065
   3.3　EMUs Body Maintenance ··· 071

Chapter 4　EMUs Bogie Structure and Maintenance ······················ 083

   4.1　Bogie Design Principles ·· 083
   4.2　The Composition of Bogie ·· 084
   4.3　Maintenance of EMUs Bogie ··· 117

Chapter 5　EMUs End Connection Device Structure and Maintenance ······ 127

   5.1　EMUs End Connection Device Structure ······························ 127
   5.2　Action Principle of EMUs Coupler ······································ 132
   5.3　EMUs Coupler Maintenance ··· 134

参考文献 ·· 138

Chapter 1

Recognizing EMUs

Learning objectives

- Know the high-speed trains of various countries;
- Recognize the different types of EMUs;
- Understand Chinese high speed train numbering rules;
- Become familiar with the components of EMUs.

1.1 High-Speed Trains Around the World

1.1.1 High–Speed Trains in Japan

The Shinkansen is a high-speed railway system in Japan and the first high-speed railway system in the world to be put into commercial operation. It uses a standard 1435 mm gauge and operates purely passenger services. Initially, it was built to connect distant Japanese regions with Tokyo, the capital, to aid economic growth and development. Beyond long-distance travel, some sections around the largest metropolitan areas are used as a commuter rail network. The first line was the Tokaido Shinkansen between Tokyo and Osaka. It was opened to traffic on October 1st, 1964 before the start of the Tokyo Olympics. After years of expansion, there are currently 9 lines, including 2 shorter lines. The "mini Shinkansen" connect the most important cities in Japan. It was originally developed and operated by the Japanese state-owned railways, and after the division and privatization of the National Railways, it was continued by the JR Group. Currently, there are 5 JR companies providing services, including JR Hokkaido, JR East Japan, JR Tokai, JR West Japan and JR Kyushu.

The Shinkansen is designed to be take account of load capacity and high speed.

Therefore, its construction and operation technology are different from traditional railways. For example, Shinkansen trains use decentralized power, three-dimensional intersections and were the first trains to use an automatic train control system. The departure interval time of Shinkansen trains can be as low as 3 min. Bar the mini Shinkansen, the trains can reach a maximum speed of 240 to 320 km/h depending on the line. However during the speed test, it set a record of 443 km/h (set by the "300X" experimental train in 1996), and a world record 603 km/h for SC Maglev trains in April 2015. As an important symbol of Japan's top railway technology across the globe, Shinkansen technology is exported overseas.

Japan's Shinkansen network had the highest number of annual passengers (353 million in 2007) of any high-speed rail network until 2011, when the Chinese high-speed railway network surpassed it at 370 million passengers annually, reaching over 2.3 billion annual passengers by 2019.

There are 15 types of Shinkansen train in Japan, among them are the 0 series, 500 series, 700 series, E2-1000 models.

1.1.1.1　0 Series Shinkansen

The 0 series trains (Fig.1.5) were the first generation Shinkansen train sets built to run on Japan's Tokaido Shinkansen high-speed line which opened in 1964. Their maximum operating speed was 220 km/h. More than 3 200 cars were built. The design of the 0 series trains was very innovative and speedy at the time. The front of the train looked similar to that of a passenger plane and the trains were painted in a simple yet striking blue and white. The last remaining train sets were withdrawn in 2008.

Fig.1.5　0 Series Shinkansen

1.1.1.2　500 Series Shinkansen

The 500 series is a Shinkansen high-speed train type operated by the West Japan Railway Company (JR-West) on the Tokaido Shinkansen and Sanyo Shinkansen lines in Japan since 1997. They were designed to be capable of speeds of up to 320 km/h but operated at 300 km/h , until they were finally retired from the primary Nozomi service in 2010. The train sets were then refurbished and downgraded to the all-stations Kodama service between Shin-Osaka and Hakata.

The 500 series (Fig.1.6) running gear utilizes computer-controlled active suspension for a smoother, safer ride and yaw dampers are fitted between cars for improved stability. All sixteen cars in each original train set were powered, giving a maximum of 18.24 MW. Each train cost an estimated 5 billion yen and only nine were built. It used bio-mimicry to reduce energy consumption by 15%, increase speeds by 10% and reduce noise levels while increasing passenger comfort. This was done by designing the front of the train in the shape of a kingfisher's beak.

Fig.1.6　500 Series Shinkansen

1.1.1.3　700 Series Shinkansen

The 700 series is a Japanese Shinkansen high-speed train type built between 1997 and 2006, which entered service in 1999. Originally designated as "N300" during the development phase, they formed the next generation of Shinkansen vehicles jointly designed by JR Central and JR West for use on the Tokaido Shinkansen, Hakata Minami Line and the Sanyo Shinkansen. Though it has since been withdrawn from service on the Tokaido Shinkansen, the 700 series still operates on the Sanyo Shinkansen and Hakata Minami Line.

The 700 series is characterized by its flat "duck-bill" nose designed to reduce the piston effect when the trains enter tunnels. The 16-car units are painted white with blue stripes beneath the windows and are used for the Nozomi and Kodama services on the Tokaido and Sanyo Shinkansen lines, while 8-car units are used for the Sanyo Shinkansen services and have a darker livery which also acts to visually deemphasize the units' nose area, resulting in a more streamlined impression.

As with the 500 series trains, yaw dampers are fitted between vehicles, and all cars feature semi-active suspension to ensure smooth ride characteristics at high speed. Compared with the small fleet of high-performance, high-cost 500 series trains built for JR-West, these trains were designed to give improved ride comfort and interior ambience over the earlier 300 series trains at a lower cost than the 500 series trains. The cost of a 16-car 700 series unit is approximately 4 billion yen compared with around 5 billion yen for a 16-car 500 series train.

Fig.1.7　700 Series Shinkansen

1.1.1.4　E2-1000 Series Shinkansen

The E2 series is a Japanese high-speed Shinkansen train type operated by the East

Japan Railway Company (JR East) introduced to the Tohoku Shinkansen high-speed lines in Japan in 1997. The E2 series was formed in 8 and 10-car sets. The 8-car sets were used on the Hokuriku Shinkansen, and the 10-car sets were used on Tohoku Shinkansen services. The 10-car sets could be coupled to E3 series Komachi sets using couplers hidden behind retracting nose doors. They operated at a maximum speed of 275 km/h on the Tohoku Shinkansen. A total of 502 vehicles were built between 1997 and 2010, with the first withdrawals commencing in late 2013.

The E2-1000 series (Fig.1.8) incorporated a number of design improvements compared with the earlier series, the most noticeable of which is the change from small windows for each seating bay to wide windows similar to the E4 series trains. A new single-arm pantograph design was used with an aerofoil-shaped mounting that eliminates the need for pantograph shrouds. Withdrawals of E2-1000 series sets commenced in March 2019.

Fig.1.8　E2-1000 Series Shinkansen

All Shinkansen trains adopt a decentralized drive mode to prevent hunting motion at high speed and to reduce the maintenance cost of the line. When driving the vibration is extremely small, and the overall running quality is excellent.

Comparison of Various Types of EMUs in Japan is shown in Tab.1.2.

Tab.1.2 Comparison of Various Types of EMUs in Japan

Shinkansen operating trains over the years							
Model	V_{max}/(km/h)	1960s	1970s	1980s	1990s	2000s	2010s
0series	220	1964 – 2008					
100series	230				1985 – 2012		
300series	270				1992 – 2012		
500series	300					1997 – now	
700series	285					1999 – now	
800series	260					2004 – now	
N700series	300					2007	
N700Sseries	300						2020 – now
L0series	505						2027 (project)
200series	240			1982 – 2013			
400series	240				1992 – 2010		
E1series	240				1994 – 2012		
E2series	275					1997 – now	
E3series	275					1997 – now	
E4series	240					1997 – 2021	
E5series·H5series	320						2011 – now
E6series	320						2013 – now
E7series·W7series	260						2014 – now
E8series	300				2024 (Project)			
Operator		Japan National Railways (1964 – 1987)			JR companies (1987 – now)			

1.1.2 High-Speed Trains in Germany

The Intercity Express (ICE) refers to the system of high-speed trains predominantly running in Germany. It also serves some destinations in Austria, Denmark, France, Belgium, Switzerland and the Netherlands mostly as part of cross border service. It is the highest service category of rail and the flagship train of the German state railway, the Deutsche Bahn. There are currently 259 train sets in operation. ICE trains are the highest category trains in the fare system of the Deutsche Bahn. Their fares are not calculated on a fixed per-kilometer table as with other trains, but instead have fixed prices for station-to-station connections, levied on the grounds that the ICE trains have a higher level of comfort. Travelling at speeds of up to 320 km/h, they are tailored for business travelers or long-distance commuters and are marketed by the Deutsche Bahn as an alternative to flights.

Apart from domestic use, the trains can also be found in countries neighboring Germany. There are ICE 1 lines to Basel and Zurich. ICE 3 trains also run to Liège and Brussels and at lower speeds to Amsterdam. On June 10th, 2007, a new line between Paris and Frankfurt/Stuttgart was opened, jointly operated by ICE and TGV trains.

The Deutsche Bahn started a series of trials in 1985 using the Inter City Experimental (ICE-V) test train. The ICE-V was used as a showcase train and for high-speed trials, setting a new world speed record of 406.9 km/h on May 1st, 1988. The train was retired in 1996 and replaced with a new trial unit, called the ICE-S.

1.1.2.1 First Generation ICE 1

The first ICE trains were the ICE 1 train sets (Fig.1.9), which came into service in 1989. The first regularly scheduled ICE trains ran from June 1991 from Hamburg – Altona to Munich at hourly intervals. The Hanover – Würzburg line and the Mannheim – Stuttgart line, which had both opened the same year, were hence integrated into the ICE network from the very beginning.

Fig.1.9　ICE 1

1.1.2.2 Second Generation ICE 2

The successor ICE 2 trains (Fig.1.10), the ICE 2, went to operation in 1997. The trains were pulled by Class 402 power heads. One key design features of ICE 2 trains was the improved load balancing which was achieved by building smaller train units which could be coupled or detached as needed.

These train sets were used on the ICE line 10 Berlin – Cologne/Bonn. However, since the driving van trailers of the trains were still awaiting approval, the Deutsche Bahn joined two portions to form a long train, similar to the ICE 1. Only in May 1998 were the ICE 2 units fully equipped with driving van trailers and could be portioned on their run from Hamm via either the stations at Dortmund, Essen, Duisburg, Düsseldorf or Hagen Wuppertal, Solingen-Ohligs.

In late 1998, the Hanover – Berlin high-speed railway was opened, which became the third high-speed line in Germany, cutting travel time on line 10 by 2.5 h.

The ICE 1 and ICE 2 trains' loading gauge exceeds that recommended by the international railway organization (UIC). Even though the trains were originally intended to be used only domestically, some units are licensed to run in Switzerland and Austria. Some ICE 1 units have been equipped with an additional smaller pantograph to be able to run on the different Swiss overhead wire layout. All ICE 1 and ICE 2 trains are single-voltage AC 15 kV, which restricts their radius of operation largely to the German-speaking countries of Europe. ICE 2 trains can run at a top speed of 280 km/h.

Fig.1.10   ICE 2

1.1.2.3   Third Generation ICE 3

To overcome the restrictions imposed on the ICE 1 and ICE 2, their successor, the ICE 3 (Fig.1.11), was built with a smaller loading gauge to permit usability throughout the entire European standard gauge network, with the sole exception being the UK's domestic railway network. Unlike their predecessors, the ICE 3 units are built not as trains with separate passenger and power cars, but as electric multiple units with underfloor motors throughout. This also reduced the load per axle and enabled the ICE 3 to comply with the pertinent UIC standard.

Two different classes were developed: the Class 403 (domestic ICE 3) and the Class 406 (ICE 3M), the M standing for multi-system. The trains were branded and marketed as the **Velaro** by their manufacturer, Siemens. The latest generation ICE 3, Class 407, is known as the New ICE 3, and is part of the Siemens **Velaro** family with the model designation **Velaro D**. It currently runs on many lines in Germany and through to other countries like France.

Just like the ICE 2, the ICE 3 and the ICE 3M were developed as short trains, and are able to travel in a system where individual units run on different lines, then being coupled to travel together. Since the ICE 3 trains are the only ones able to run on the Köln – Frankfurt high-speed line with its 4.0% incline, they are used predominantly on service that utilize this line.

The high-speed line in Germany, the Erfurt – Leipzig/Halle high-speed railway, which opened in December 2015, is the most recent addition to the ICE network. It is one of the three lines in Germany (the other two are Nuremberg – Ingolstadt high – speed rail line and Cologne – Frankfurt high-speed rail line), which are equipped with a line speed of 300 km/h. Since only 3rd generation ICE trains can travel at this speed, the ICE line 41, formerly running from Essen to Nuremberg, was extended over the Nuremberg – Ingolstadt high-speed rail line. In France, the ICE 3 runs at speeds of up to 320 km/h on the LGV Est railway Strasbourg – Paris.

Fig.1.11　ICE 3

1.1.2.4 Fourth Generation ICE 4

Whereas ICE 3 has traditionally focused on increasing speed, ICE 4 (Fig.1.12) has a slightly more modest top speed and a focus on economics. Initially called ICX, it was renamed to ICE 4 in December 2015. The 12-car train ICE 4 has a total length of 346 m, a maximum speed of 250 km/h, and a total of 830 seats (205 seats in 1st class, 625 seats in 2nd class).

Fig.1.12　ICE 4

Comparison of Various Types of EMUs in Germany is shown in Tab.1.3.

Tab.1.3　Comparison of Various Types of EMUs in Germany

Type	Power/kW	V_{max} /(km/h)	Marshalling	In service
ICE 1	9600	280	2M12T	Since 1990
ICE 2	4800	280	1M7T	Since 1996
ICE 3	8000	330	4M4T	Since 2000
ICE 4	9900	250	6M6T	Since 2017

1.1.3　High Speed Trains in France

The TGV is France's intercity high-speed rail service, operated by the French National Railways. The French National Railways worked on a high-speed rail network from 1966 to 1974 and presented the project for approval. Originally it was planned for the TGV to be propelled by gas turbines, selected for their small size, good power-to-weight ratio and ability to deliver high power over an extended period. The first prototype, TGV 001, was the only gas-turbine TGV: following the oil price increase during the 1973 energy crisis, gas turbines were deemed uneconomic and the project turned to electricity from overhead lines, generated by new nuclear power stations. Changing the TGV to electric traction required a significant design overhaul. The first electric prototype, nicknamed Zébulon, was completed in 1974, and it was used to test features such as innovative body mounting of motors, pantographs, suspension and braking. Body mounting of motors allowed over 3 tonnes to be eliminated from the power cars and greatly reduced the unsprung weight. The prototype travelled almost 1 000 000 km during testing.

Following the inaugural service between Paris and Lyon in 1981 on the LGV Sud-Est (LGV for Ligne à Grande Vitesse; "high-speed line"), the network, centered on Paris, expanded to connect major cities across France including Marseille, Lille, Bordeaux, Strasbourg, Rennes and Montpellier and in neighboring countries on a combination of high-speed and conventional lines. The TGV network in France carries about 110 million passengers a year.

The high-speed tracks, maintained by the French National Railways are subject to heavy regulation. Confronted with the fact that train drivers would not be able to see signals along the track-side when trains reached full speed, engineers developed the TVM cab-signaling technology, which would later be exported worldwide. It allows for a train engaging in emergency braking to request within seconds all following trains to reduce their speed, if a driver does not react within 1.5 km, the system overrides the controls and reduces the train's speed automatically. The TVM safety mechanism enables TGVs using the same line to depart every three minutes.

A TGV test train set the world record for the fastest wheeled train, reaching a speed of 574.8 km/h, in April 2007. Conventional TGV services operate up to 320 km/h on the LGV Est, LGV Rhin-Rhône and LGV Méditerranée. In 2007, the world's fastest scheduled rail journey was a start-to-stop average speed of 279.4 km/h between the Champagne-Ardenne and Gare de Lorrain on the LGV Est, not surpassed until 2013, when the express service on the Shijiazhuang to Zhengzhou segment of China's Shijiazhuang – Wuhan high-speed railway recorded average speeds of 283.7 km/h.

The TGV system extends to neighboring countries, directly including linking (Italy, Spain, Belgium, Luxembourg and Germany) and through TGV-derivative networks which links France to Switzerland, to Belgium, Germany and the Netherlands, as well as to the United Kingdom (Eurostar). Several future lines are planned, including extensions within France and to surrounding countries.

TGVs have semi-permanently coupled articulated unpowered coaches, with Jacobs bogies between the coaches supporting both of them. Power cars at each end of the trains have their own bogies. Trains can be lengthened by coupling two TGVs, using couplers hidden in the noses of the power cars. The articulated design is advantageous during a derailment, as the passenger carriages are more likely to stay upright and in line with the track. Normal trains could split at couplings and jackknife, as seen in the Eschede train disaster. A disadvantage is that it is difficult to split sets of carriages. While power cars can be removed from trains by standard uncoupling procedures, specialized depot equipment is needed to split carriages, by lifting the entire train at once. Once uncoupled, one of the carriage ends is left without a bogie at the split, so a bogie frame is required to support it. Using power cars instead of Electric Multiple Units (EMU) easily allows for a high ride quality and less electrical equipment.

There are five types of TGV equipment in use:

1.1.3.1　The TGV Atlantic (TGV-A)

The TGV Atlantic (TGV-A) is a class of high-speed trains used in France by the French National Railways, which were built by Alstom between 1988 and 1992. Numbered 301-405, the TGV-A trains were built for the opening of the LGV Atlantic (Fig.1.13). Entry into service began in 1989. TGV-A trains are 237.5-m-long and 2.904-m-wide. They weigh 444 tonnes and are made up of two power cars and ten carriages with a total of 485 seats. They were built for a maximum speed of 300 km/h with 8 800 kW total power under 25 kV.

Fig.1.13　TGV Atlantic (TGV-A)

1.1.3.2 TGV Reseau (TGV-R)

The TGV Reseau (TGV-R) trains were built by Alstom between 1992 and 1996. This model of TGV train is based on the earlier TGV Atlantic. The first TGV-R entered service in 1993. As well as using standard French voltages of AC 25 kV and DC 1 500 V, the triple voltage sets can operate under the Belgian and Italian DC 3 kV supplies.

TGV-R are formed of two power cars (8 800 kW under 25 kV – like the TGV Atlantic) and eight carriages, giving a capacity of 377 seats. They have a top speed of 320 km/h. They are 200-m-long and are 2.904-m-wide. The dual-voltage sets weigh 383 tonnes and owing to axle-load restrictions in Belgium the triple-voltage sets have a series of modifications, such as the replacement of steel with aluminum and hollow axles, to reduce the weight to under 17 tonnes per axle. Owing to early complaints of uncomfortable pressure changes when entering tunnels at high speed on the LGV Atlantic, the TGV Reseau (Fig.1.14) trainsets is pressure-sealed.

Fig.1.14　TGV Reseau (TGV-R)

1.1.3.3 TGV Duplex

The TGV Duplex (Fig.1.15) was a French high-speed train in the TGV series, manufactured by Alstom and operated by the French National Railways. It was unique among TGV trains in that it featured bi-level carriages. The TGV Duplex inaugurated the third generation of TGV trains.

TGV Duplex trains had aluminum bodies, the strict requirement of a 17-tonne axle load limit made it imperative to cut down on weight, wherever possible. Extruded aluminum construction reduce 20% of structure weight.

The nose of the power units and the gap between trailers were improved to the extent that a Duplex train cruising at a speed of 300 km/h experienced only 4% more drag than a single-level TGV.

The active pantograph, the Faiveley CX, used on the TGV Duplex had a pneumatically actuated active control system. Two small gas cylinders in the wiper armature could tune the stiffness of the pantographs upper stage, to optimize contact at any speed.

TGV Duplex trains had all wheel disc brakes, earlier TGVs (including Eurostar) used disc brakes only on unpowered axles. Weight gains on the Duplex power units allowed the installation of disc brakes directly on the wheels of powered axles, instead of using the traditional tread brakes. This did not greatly improve braking performance, but it left the wheel tread smooth and considerably reduced rolling noise.

The cooling fans in the TGV Duplex power units produced the most noticeable sound when the train was in a station. The fans, located in the roof of the unit, were redesigned to be quieter.

The Duplex was specially designed to increase capacity on high-speed lines with saturated traffic. With two seating levels and a seating capacity of 508 passengers, the TGV Duplex increased the passenger capacity. While the TGV Duplex started as a small component of the TGV fleet, it became one of the workhorses.

Fig.1.15 TGV Duplex

1.1.3.4 TGV POS

The TGV POS (POS stands for Paris – Ostfrankreich – Süddeutschland in German, which means Paris – Eastern France – Southern Germany). The POS (Fig.1.16) is a TGV trainset built by French manufacturer Alstom which is operated by the French National Railways, on France's high-speed rail lines. It was originally ordered by the French National Railways to use on the new LGV Est, which was put into service in 2007. Each TGV POS trainset is formed of eight existing TGV Reseau single-deck carriages paired with new power cars, with a total power output of 9.6 MW and a top speed of 320 km/h under 25 kV. The surplus TGV Reseau power cars have been combined with newer TGV Duplex carriages to create TGV Reseau Duplex trainsets. This is because traffic on the LGV Est is expected to be less than on the heavily congested LGV Sud-Est. The TGV POS links France to Germany and Switzerland. In Switzerland, it travels from Basel to Zurich and on the line from Vallorbe to Lausanne coming from Paris. From 2013 to 2019, all of the TGV POS trainsets operated under the TGV Lyria brand and livery (a joint-venture by French National Railways and the Swiss Federal Railways) with services between France and Switzerland, replacing the nine TGV PSE trainsets that were taken out of service.

Each TGV POS trainset weighs 383 tonnes and is numbered in the 4400 series. The livery is the same as that of TGV Reseau sets (silver and blue). Pre-production set No 4401 had a prototype livery similar as the one used on the TGV Duplex sets but, in March 2007, the blue areas were stickered over with silver and now the sets have the same appearance as other sets. Like the TGV TMST, the TGV POS power cars have asynchronous motors and, in case of failure, isolation of an individual motor in a powered bogie is possible. By using IGBT (Insulated Gate Bipolar Transistor) power packs, the new power cars are capable of developing 75% of their full rated power under 15 kV German and Swiss electrifications, compared to 45% for existing TGV power cars. This allows POS trains to operate at the same speed as Intercity-Express trains in Germany.

Fig.1.16　TGV POS

1.1.3.5 TGV Euroduplex

The TGV Euroduplex (Fig.1.17) is a high-speed double-decker electric multiple unit train manufactured by Alstom. It is primarily operated by the French National Railways and also in operation with the Moroccan National Railways.

The Euroduplex trains are interoperable, containing equipment allowing them to travel between several European continental countries with various types of electrification and signaling systems. A Moroccan variation is the first high-speed train to operate in Africa.

The Euroduplex trains are an evolution of the TGV Duplex but also keep some of the features. The drive is a similar type to the TGV POS asynchronous traction motors, and it uses the European signaling system. The trailers feature improved information systems.

The TGV Euroduplex differs from the TGV Duplex as it has: UIC (International Union of Railways) loading gauge with more headroom upstairs, improved windows, Passenger Information System (SIVE) with voice announcements as in the TER trains, outside SIVE dynamic light display indicating the number of the train, its route and the number of the car, fixed filler gaps on all doors, overall control of each axle, improved accessibility for wheelchairs. It also has new interiors that include new seat designs in both classes, rotating seats with USB sockets in first class and individual lights are now included in the seats.

Fig.1.17 TGV Euroduplex

Comparison of Various Types of EMUs in France is shown in Tab.1.4.

Tab.1.4   Comparison of Various Types of EMUs in France

Equipment type	Top speed /(km/h)	Seating capacity	Overall length/m	Width /m	Weight empty/t	Weight full/t	Power /kW	First built
TGV Atlantic	300	485	238	2.90	444	484	8 800	1988
TGV Reseau	320	377	200	2.90	383	415	8 800	1992
TGV Duplex	320	508	200	2.90	380	424	8 800	1994
TGV POS	320	361	200	2.90	383	415	9 280	2005
TGV Euroduplex	320	509/ 533	200	2.90	380	424	9 400	2011

1.1.4   High Speed Trains in China

China's EMUs include the CRH (China Railway Highspeed) series and CR (China Railway) series. The CRH series is divided into the CRH1, CRH2, CRH3, CRH5 and other series models. The name CRHs was introduced in 2007. CRH trains are produced according to China's actual needs on the basis of introducing foreign EMUs technology. It is an EMUs with independent innovation significance. Subsequently, CRH380 series EMUs were successively developed and manufactured. The CR series EMUs were independently developed by China in 2012 and named CR in 2017. CR trains are EMUs with independent intellectual property rights and are a bright business card for China's high-speed rail technology export to the international market. CR EMUs include the CR400, CR300 and CR200 speed series models (including intelligent EMU).

1.1.4.1   CRH series – CRH1A platform EMUs

The CRH1A platform EMUs is manufactured in China and incorporates BSP technology from Bombardier Sifang (Qingdao) Transportation Ltd. (BST) and has speed grades of 200 km/h and 250 km/h. The CRH1A platform EMUs includes the following trainsets; CRH1A (8 Marshalling, 5M+3T), CRH1A-A (8 Marshalling, 5M+3T), CRH1B (16 Marshalling, 10M+6T) and CRH1E (sleeper EMUs, 16 Marshalling, 10M+ 6T). Some of these EMUs are shown in Fig.1.18 and Fig.1.19. CRH1A platform EMUs mainly operate in Shanghai, Jiangxi Province, Guangdong Province, Sichuan Province and other regions.

Fig.1.18　CRH1A EMUs

Fig.1.19　CRH1E EMUs

1.1.4.2　CRH series – CRH2A platform EMUs

The CRH2A platform EMUs used the Kawasaki Heavy Industry E2-1000 EMUs from Japan as its prototype. The CRH2A platform EMUs was independently innovated and developed by CRRC Qingdao Sifang Locomotive & Rolling Stock Co., Ltd. As shown in

Fig.1.20. The CRH2A platform EMUs consists of the following trainsets; CRH2A (8 Marshalling, 4M+4T), CRH2B (16 Marshalling, 8M+8T), CRH2C (8 Marshalling, 6M+2T), CRH2E (sleeper EMUs, 16 Marshalling, 8M+8T), CRH2G (cold resistant, 8 Marshalling 4M+4T) and CRH2J (comprehensive inspection trains, 8 Marshalling, 4M+4T). The maximum operating speed of the CRH2C EMUs is 300 km/h and for other types of CRH2 EMUs is 250 km/h. The CRH2G is a specialized cold and sand/windstorm resistant version. This type of EMUs has been put into operation in northwest and southwest regions of China, on high-speed rail lines such as Lanzhou – Xinjiang, Xi'an – Lanzhou and Kunming – Dali – Lijiang. CRH2A platform EMUs are mainly operate in Shanxi Province, Hubei Province, Shaanxi Province, Shandong Province, Shanghai City, Jiangxi Province, Guangdong Province, Sichuan Province, Guangxi Province and Yunnan Province.

Fig.1.20　CRH2A EMUs

1.1.4.3　CRH series – CRH3 platform EMUs

The CRH3 platform EMUs is mainly manufactured by CRRC Tangshan Co., Ltd. The maximum operating speed of the CRH3A (8 Marshalling, 4M+4T) is 250 km/h. The CRH3A EMUs (Fig.1.21) is suitable for long ramp operation, mainly in Liaoning Province and Sichuan Province. The CRH3C (8 Marshalling, 4M and 4T) as the first generation of typical EMUs, was independently developed using the German ICE-3 train as a prototype and has a maximum operating speed of 350 km/h. It mainly operates on lines in Guangdong Province and Sichuan Province.

Fig.1.21 CRH3A EMUs

1.1.4.4 CRH Series – CRH5A platform EMUs

The CRH5A platform EMUs is produced by CRRC Changchun Railway Vehicles Co., Ltd. It has 8 marshalling with a maximum operating speed of 250 km/h, it includes the trainsets; CRH5A (8 Marshalling, 5M+3T), CRH5G (Fig.1.22, cold and sand/windstorm resistant, 8 Marshalling, 5M+3T), CRH5E (sleeper trains, 16 Marshalling, 10M+6T) and CRH5J (Comprehensive inspection train, 8 Marshalling, 5M+3T), which mainly operate in northern China.

Fig.1.22 CRH5G EMUs

1.1.4.5 CRH380 Series – CRH380A Platform EMUs

The CRH380A platform EMUs is a high-speed EMUs independently developed by CRRC Qingdao Sifang Locomotive & Rolling Stock Co., Ltd. using the CRH2C EMUs as a foundation and has a maximum operating speed of 350 km/h. The CRH380A platform EMUs includes the; CRH380A (8 marshalling, 6M+ 2T), CRH380AL (Fig 1.23, 16 marshalling, 14M+2T), CRH380AN (8 marshalling, 6M+2T), CRH380AJ (Comprehensive inspection train, 8 marshalling, 7M+1T) and CRH380AM (Comprehensive inspection train, 6M).

Fig.1.23 CRH380AL EMUs

1.1.4.6 CRH380 Series – CRH380B Platform EMUs

The CRH380B platform EMUs is one of the CRH380 series high-speed EMUs independently developed by CRRC Tangshan Co., Ltd. and CRRC Changchun Railway Vehicles Co., Ltd. using the CRH3C EMUs as a foundation, it includes the following trainsets; CRH 380B (8 marshalling, 4M+4T), CRH380BL (16 marshalling, 8M+8T), CRH380BG (cold resistant, 8 marshalling, 4M+4T) and CRH380BJ (comprehensive inspection train, 8M marshalling, 4M+4T) and CRH380BJ-A (cold resistant comprehensive inspection train, 8 formation, 4M+4T). The CRH380B platform EMUs has a maximum operating speed of 350 km/h and is shown in Fig.1.24. The CRH380BG EMUs is a cold resistant EMUs independently developed by CRRC Changchun Railway Vehicles Co., Ltd. Using the CRH380BL EMUs as a foundation.

Fig.1.24 CRH380B EMUs

1.1.4.7 CRH380 Series – CRH380C Platform EMUs

The CRH380C platform EMUs is produced by CRRC Changchun Railway Vehicles Co., Ltd. and is a type of CRH380CL EMUs (16 marshalling, 8M+8T), with a maximum operating speed of 350 km/h, which is shown in Fig.1.25.

Fig.1.25 CRH380CL EMUs

1.1.4.8 CRH380 Series – CRH380D Platform EMUs

The CRH380D platform EMUs is a CRH380 series high speed EMUs developed by Bombardier Sifang (Qingdao) Transportation Ltd. (BST). It is a type of CRH380D EMUs (8 marshalling, 4M+4T). Its highest operating speed is 350 km/h and is shown in Fig.1.26.

Fig.1.26 CRH380D EMUs

1.1.4.9 CR Series

CR series EMUs are Chinese Standard EMUs developed by the China State Railway Group Co., Ltd., with completely independent intellectual property rights and are some of the most technologically advanced EMUs in the world. The CR400 EMUs is currently the highest operating high-speed train in the world. CR series EMUs include the CR400, CR300 and CR200. 400 means the EMUs has been designed to operate at the speed of 300 to 400 km/h, 300 means the EMUs has been designed to operate at the speed of 200 to 300 km/h; 200 means the EMUs has been designed to operate at the speed of 100 to 200 km/h.

In June 2017, China's standard EMUs was officially named "Fuxing Hao" and began operating on the Beijing – Shanghai, Beijing – Tianjin, Beijing – Guangzhou, Shanghai – Nanjing and other high-speed railway lines. In order to meet the transportation needs of large passenger flow trunk lines, 16 and 17 marshalling "Fuxing Hao" EMUs have been put into operation one after another.

1.1.4.10 CR Series – CR400 platform EMUs

The CR400 platform EMUs is divided into two platforms: the CR400AF platform EMUs and the CR400BF platform EMUs. The CR400AF platform EMUs is designed by CRRC Qingdao Sifang Locomotive & Rolling Stock Co., Ltd., and manufactured by CRRC Qingdao Sifang Locomotive & Rolling Stock Co., Ltd. and BST Company respectively. It includes the CR400AF (8marshallings, 4M+4T), CR400AF-A (16marshallings, 8M+8T), CR400AF-B (17marshallings, 8M+9T) and CR400AF-G (cold resistant, 8marshallings 4M+4T) EMUs. The CR400BF platform EMUs is designed by CRRC Changchun Railway Vehicles Co., Ltd. and manufactured by CRRC Changchun Railway Vehicles Co., Ltd. and CRRC Tangshan Co., Ltd. It includes the CR400BF-B (17marshallings, 8M+9T) and CR400BF-G (cold resistant, 8marshallings, 4M+4T). CR400AF and CR400BF platform EMUs can achieve interconnection.

CR400AF EMUs and CR400BF EMUs are shown as in Fig.1.27.

Fig.1.27　CR400AF EMUs and CR400BF EMUs

1.1.4.11 CR Series – CR300 platform EMUs

On the basis of the successful development of the CR400 "FuXing Hao" with a speed of 350 km/h, China continued to develop the CR300 "FuXing Hao" EMUs with a speed of 250 km/h. In November 2019, CRRC Qingdao Sifang Locomotive & Rolling Stock Co., Ltd. and CRRC Changchun Railway Vehicles Co., Ltd. obtained the model license and manufacturing license of CR300AF (8marshallings, 4M+4T) and CR300BF (8marshallings, 4M+4T) "Fuxing Hao" with a speed of 250km/h issued by China State Railway Group Co., Ltd, as shown in Fig.1.28. It has been put into operation in the regional railway network passenger dedicated line.

Fig.1.28　CR300AF EMUs (left) and CR400BF EMUs (right)

1.1.4.12　CR Series – CR200J EMUs

The difference between the CR200J EMUs and the above EMUs is that the CR200J EMUs is a power centralized EMUs. Power centralized EMUs are also an important part of the "Fuxing Hao" EMUs series. The 160 km/h power centralized EMUs is widely used on existing lines in China, and the CR200J can operate normally at a speed of 160 km/h on Passenger Dedicated Lines (PDL) with the a speed limit of over 200 km/h. Both ends of the CR200J are equipped with cabs. CR200J EMUs are divided into long and short marshaling in which the long marshalling train is 11-20marshalings (2M+(9~18)T), and the short marshalling train is 9marshalings (1M+9T). The CR200J is jointly produced by CRRC Tangshan Co., Ltd., CRRC Puzhen Co., Ltd., CRRC Changchun Railway Vehicles Co., Ltd. and CRRC Qingdao Sifang Locomotive & Rolling Stock Co., Ltd.

1.2　Types of EMUs

1.2.1　Classification by Traction Power Type

According to the type of traction power, trains are divided into electric multiple units (EMUs), diesel multiple units (DMUs), hybrid trains (EEMUs&DEMUs) and maglev trains.

1. EMUs

EMUs refer to trains running on electrified railways. Because the electric power is extracted from the outside as the energy source, the power structure is omitted, so the electric traction has the advantages of large traction power, light axle weight, good economy, and environmental protection. Thus 80% of high-speed railways across the world use electric traction. China's high-speed EMUs have absolute advantages in the world in terms of quantity and quality, and the proportion of electrified traction is higher in China than in ofher countries. The EMUs mentioned in this book are electric power decentralized multiple units.

2. DMUs

DMUs refers to a train driven by an internal combustion engine. According to the type of internal combustion engine, it can also be divided into diesel train and gas turbine train. The vast majority of China's railway diesel trains are DMUs. DMUs have the advantages of low investment and quick results, so they are usually used in high-speed railway sections that have not yet been electrified or as a bridge for the development of high-speed railway construction. At present, DMUs are rarely used in China, and Passenger Dedicated Lines are not used.

3. Hybrid trains

Hybrid trains are driven by a variety of motive power sources (catenary, battery, internal combustion engine). They can meet the needs of cross-line operation from electrified railways to non-electrified railways, providing passengers with convenient travel. Hybrid trains include; battery-electric catenary-powered (EEMU) and catenary-powered internal combustion engine (DEMU). At present, hybrid trains have not been officially put into commercial operation in China.

4. Maglev trains

Maglev trains are not used on a large scale. They use electromagnetic system to suspend the whole train on a guide rail and use a linear motor to directly convert the electric energy into traction force to drive the train to run at high speed. Maglev trains are suitable for ultra-high-speed operation because the wheels and rails do not make contact and have no frictional resistance. The top speed of a maglev train is over 500 km/h, and its maximum test speed is 581 km/h. At present, China has successfully introduced low-speed maglev trains into commercial operation and high-speed maglev trains are still under development and testing.

1.2.2 Classification by Power Distribution Method

The power distribution method refers to the number and location of power units in the EMUs marshalling. EMUs can be divided into power centralized and power decentralized according to their power distribution method.

1. Power centralized EMUs

In EMUs marshalling, the power distribution method with power units at both ends (or power unit at one end and control unit at the other end) and trailers in the middle is called power centralized EMUs. The utility model is characterized in that the power units at both ends are a complete power unit, which is different from the traditional centralized power locomotive, which can only traction without carrying passengers. The power unit and the control unit can properly accommodate the drivers and passengers. The control unit is also equipped with a driver's cab, the driver's cab has an aerodynamic design.

Compared with a power decentralized train, a power centralized train has a lighter power unit and it is easier to maintain, but the disadvantage is that the motor train has a larger axle load. The CR200 series EMUs in China, TGV Series in France and ICE1, ICE2 series in Germany are all power centralized trains.

2. Power decentralized EMUs

The power distribution method of power decentralized EMUs means that all cars are power cars, or some are power cars and the others are trailers. Power units are formed by two or more cars (as shown in Fig.1.29) and the power wheels driven by the motor are distributed under all or some of the cars. The transformers and converters in the power unit are suspended in different places. Under the car, the power unit can also be hung on the lower part of the train, so that the axle load of the EMUs is relatively uniform, and the entire EMUs can be composed of several power units.

Compared with the power centralized EMUs, the power decentralized EMUs have the following advantages: they are composed of multiple power units and have a high redundancy; the number of powered axles is large, the adhesion requirement is low and they are less affected by environmental conditions and climate; the traction equipment is installed under the floor, the axle weight is light and evenly distributed and they have little impact on the railways. On the other hand, there are also disadvantages such as a large number of power units and a large amount of maintenance.

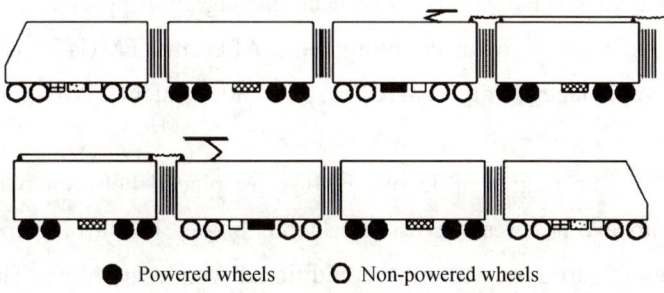

Fig.1.29 Power Decentralized EMUs

1.2.3 Classification by Speed Class

According to speed class, an EMUs can be divided into ordinary speed, fast, high-speed and ultra-high-speed.

(1) Ordinary Speed EMUs: Operating speed of 80 – 160 km/h; are used in subways, existing lines, mixed passenger and freight lines and suburban lines.

(2) Fast EMUs: Operating speed of 160 – 200 km/h; are mainly used in intercity railways.

(3) High-speed EMUs: Operating speed of 200 – 400 km/h; further subdivided into 200 – 250 km/h, 300 – 400 km/h passenger dedicated lines, which are used in regional railway network and passenger dedicated lines.

(4) Ultra-high-speed EMUs: Top speed is greater than 400 km/h in the next step of development, trial operation and planning. Such as the maglev train.

1.2.4 Classification by EMUs Bogie Type

EMUs are classified according to the type of bogie they use. There are two types of bogie: the independent bogie and the Jacobs bogie as shown in Fig.1.30.

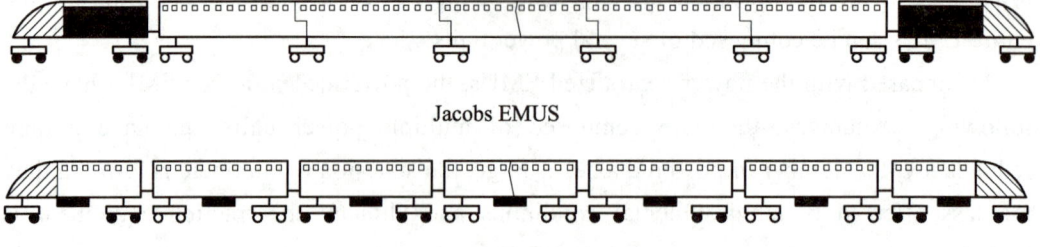

Fig.1.30 Classification by EMUs Bogie Type

Independent EMUs: The train body of each carriage is supported by two bogies, and the carriages are connected by a coupling part. After the EMUs is disassembled, the carriage can move independently. Therefore, the independent EMUs is convenient for maintenance.

Jacobs EMUs: The bogies of Jacobs EMUs are placed between two carriages. The weight of each carriage is spread across the Jacobs bogie. This arrangement provides the smooth ride of bogie carriages without the additional weight and drag. The advantages of Jacobs EMUs are: safety, because the trains are less prone to collapse like an accordion after derailing; lower weight and simpler and cheaper construction because bogies are heavy, expensive and complex structures, less rail squeal and other wheel-to-rail noise because of fewer bogies. French TGV trains are Jacobs EMUs, and China high-speed trains are independent EMUs.

There are many classification methods for EMUs. In practical application, EMUs often have the respective characteristics of the above classifications. The naming of EMUs also includes multi-parameter factors such as speed grade, enterprise identification code, technical specification code, technology type code, etc. The naming method for EMUs is described in the next section.

1.3 EMUs Numbering Rules in China

There are many types of EMUs and the number of EMUs and the naming of EMUs types need to be standardized in a complete way. Fig.1.31 shows the numbering of EMUs in China.

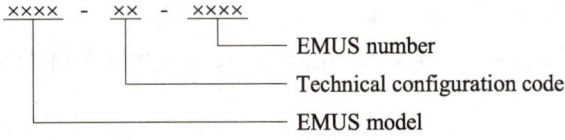

Fig.1.31 Numbering of EMUs in China

1.3.1 EMUs Models

The naming method of Chinese EMUs models in the CR series and CRH series is generally similar, but there are a few differences. They are introduced below.

1. EMUs models in CR series

The model and technical specification codes of EMUs in the CR series are shown in Fig.1.32.

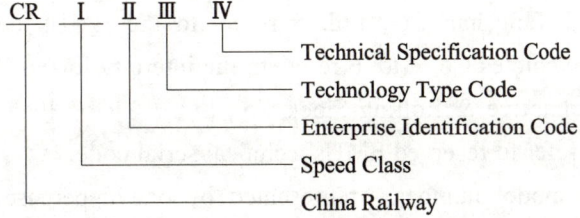

Fig.1.32 Model and Technical Specification Codes of CR EMUs Series

Ⅰ: Speed class - represented by three Arabic numerals, for example; 400 - means the design running speed is 300 to 400 km/h; 300 - means the design running speed is 200 to 300 km/h; 200 - means the design running speed is 100 to 200 km/h.

Ⅱ: Enterprise identification code - represented by one uppercase English letter and arranged in order starting from A. A represents the EMUs developed by CRRC Qingdao Sifang Locomotive & Rolling Stock Co., Ltd. B represents the EMUs developed by CRRC Changchun Railway Vehicles Co., Ltd. the rest of the letters are reserved.

Ⅲ: Technology type code - represented by a single capital letter, such as F, J, N, P and other letters: F stands for power decentralized EMUs; J stands for power centralized EMUs; N stands for power centralized internal combustion EMUs; P stands for power decentralized internal-combustion EMUs. The rest of the letters are reserved.

Ⅳ: Technical specification code - represented by one to two capital letters. The technical specification code of the basic product of each model is default and the other technical specification codes are arranged starting from A. It is a general improved product to distinguish different marshalling types, different capacity, different EMUs types and the adaptability of the same model.

2. EMUs models in CRH series

The model and technical specification codes of CRH EMUs series are shown in Fig.1.33.

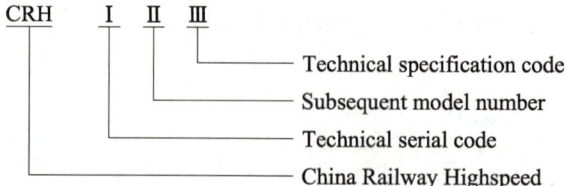

Fig.1.33 Model and Technical Specification Codes of CR EMUs Series

Ⅰ: Technical serial code - represented by Arabic numerals, arranged in order starting from 1. Used to represent the enterprise of EMUs. 1 refers to the EMUs developed by Bombardier Sifang (Qingdao) Transportation Ltd. 2 refers to the EMUs developed by CRRC Qingdao Sifang Locomotive & Rolling Stock Co., Ltd. 3 refers to the EMUs developed by CRRC Tangshan Co., Ltd. 5 refers to the EMUs developed by CRRC Changchun Railway Vehicles Co., Ltd. 6 refers to the intercity EMUs developed by CRRC Qingdao Sifang Locomotive & Rolling Stock Co., Ltd. / CRRC Puzhen Co., Ltd., 7 and subsequent numbers refer to reserved EMUs technical serial code.

Ⅱ: Subsequent model number - represented by one uppercase English letter and arranged in order starting with A. A represents a speed of 200-250 km/h, 8 marshalling with semi-cushioned seats. B represents a speed of 200-250 km/h, 16 marshalling with semi-cushioned seats. C represents a speed of 300-350 km/h, 8 marshalling with semi-cushioned seats. D represents a speed of 300-350 km/h, 16 marshalling with semi-cushioned seats. E represents a speed of 200-250 km/h, 16 marshalling with sleeper. F represents a speed of 160 km/h, 8 marshalling intercity EMUs. G represents a speed of 200-250 km/h, 8 marshalling with cold resistant EMUs. H reserved; I reserved; J represents a comprehensive inspection EMUs. K and subsequent letters reserved subsequent model numbers of EMUs.

Ⅲ: Technical specification code - represented by one to two capital letters, arranged starting with A, to distinguish different technical specification under the same basic model. The technical specification code of each basic model can be defaulted.

1.3.2 EMUs Carriage Number

EMUs carriage numbers include a carriage code, manufacturers serial number and marshalling sequence code, as shown in Fig.1.34.

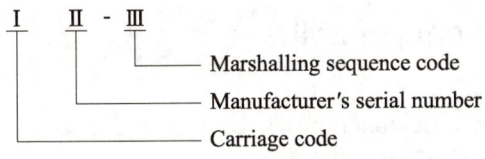

Fig.1.34　EMUs Carriage Number

Ⅰ: The carriage code of EMUs indicates the type of carriage. The carriage code of EMUs is usually an abbreviation from Chinese pinyin. The carriages are classified according to their functions, as shown in Tab.1.5.

Tab.1.5　Carriage Classification According to Function

No.	carriage code	meaning
1	ZY	First Class Coach
2	ZE	Second Class Coach
3	WR	Soft Sleeper Coach
4	WY	Hard Sleeper Coach
5	CA	Dining Coach
6	SW	Business Coach
7	ZEC	Second Class/Dining Coach
8	ZYS	First Class/Business Coach

Continue

No.	carriage code	meaning
9	ZES	Second Class/ Business Coach
10	ZYT	First Class/ Premier Coach
11	ZET	Second Class/ Premier Coach
12	JC	Detection train
13	WRC	Soft Sleeper/Dining Coach
14	WG	Luxury Sleeper coach

Ⅱ: The manufacturers serial number indicates the manufacturer and model of the EMUs carriage. The manufactures serial number is usually represented by four Arabic numerals.

Ⅲ: The marshalling sequence code is represented by two Arabic numerals and the codes from the first carriage, the second carriage to the last carriage are 01, 02 etc. There are 8 short marshalling and 16 long marshalling.

1.4 Components of EMUs

According to the specific functions of each part, the general EMUs consists of the following 8 parts: car body, bogie, traction drive and control system, braking device, end connection device, current collection device, interior equipment and train network control system as shown in Fig.1.35. Among them the car body, bogie and end connection device can be classified as the mechanical components of the EMUs. Its structure and maintenance will be introduced in detail in the next three chapters.

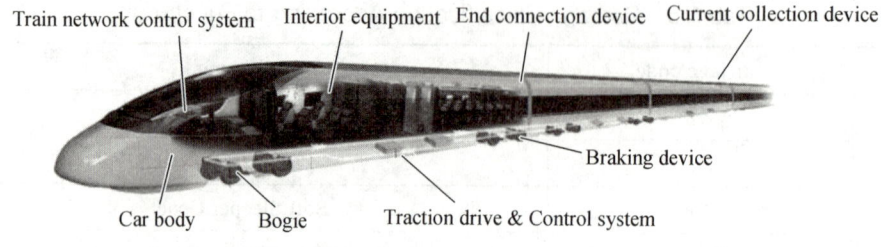

Fig.1.35　Components of EMUs

1.4.1　Car body

The car body is the part that accommodates passengers and their luggage. It is also the place where drivers cabs are located. In addition, the foundation and skeleton for installing and connecting other equipment and components can be found here, such as seat lighting equipment, sanitary facilities and air conditioning systems.

The car body usually consists of the chassis, end walls, side walls and roof and other parts. EMUs consist of two types of car body: the driver's cab and driverless car. The function of the car body is to provide passengers with a comfortable seating and standing space and to carry the train components as well as to contain the longitudinal connection load.

Modern EMUs car bodies are required to meet strength and stiffness standards while being as light as possible. Therefore, the main body is constructed with stainless steel and aluminum alloy. At this stage, carbon fiber is being tested by certain manufacturers.

Car Body Manufacturing Plant is shown as in Fig.1.36.

Fig.1.36 Car Body Manufacturing Plant

1.4.2 Bogie

Bogies are located at the lowermost part of an EMUs, between the car body and the track. They pull and guide the EMUs to travel along the track and bear and transmit various loads from the car body and the track easing its power effect; they are a key component to ensure the quality of EMUs operation and ensure the safety of operation.

Bogies are divided into motor bogies (Fig.1.37) and trailer bogies and their functions are load-bearing, guiding, damping and braking. The motor bogie also has a traction drive function.

The bogie is generally composed of a frame, a spring suspension device, a wheel set axle box device and a basic brake device. For the motor bogie, a drive device (including a traction motor and a transmission gear) is also installed.

Fig.1.37　Motor Bogie

1.4.3　Traction Drive and Control System

The traction drive and control system of the EMUs mainly refers to the electrical equipment and control circuits of the EMUs.

The function of the traction drive and control system is to realize the efficient transmission and conversion of electric energy, drive the train forward and control the normal operation of the train.

Generally, traction drive and control systems can be divided into three parts: main drive circuit system, auxiliary circuit system, electronic and control circuit system.

The main drive circuit system consists of 2 power units, each power unit consists of 1 traction transformer, 2 traction converters and 8 traction motors, each traction converter drives 4 traction motors. When the main drive circuit system fails, the single-vehicle traction or a single traction unit can be cut off without affecting other traction work. The cut off power can also be cut off by activating the high voltage isolating switch. The main drive circuit system is shown in Fig.1.38. The auxiliary circuit system components mainly include: charger, battery, electrical connector, switchboard layout and equipment, splitting phase detection system, 220 V load socket and single-phase inverter power supply, external power supply connector box, control load circuit junction box, DC 24 V power supply, fuse relay, under-vehicle insulation temperature relay, external power socket for rescue, etc. The electronic and control circuit system mainly includes various control devices related to the traction drive system.

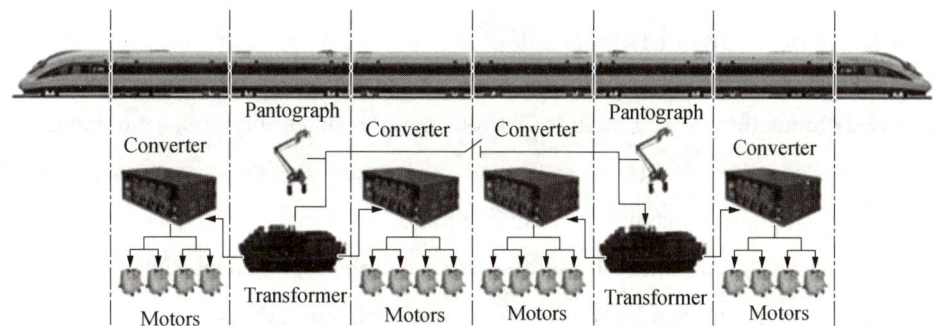

Fig.1.38 Main Drive Circuit System

1.4.4 Braking Device

The braking device includes a mechanical part, an air line part and an electric control part. Its role is to generate a certain braking force, so that the train decelerates or stops within a specified distance or time.

The braking device is an indispensable device to ensure the safe operation of the train. The braking device is not only found on the motor units, but also the trailer, so that the EMUs can be decelerated as required or parked within a prescribed distance. EMUs usually use two types of braking electric and air. Electric braking involves the conversion of the EMUs kinetic energy into electric energy by cutting the magnetic field line of the motor and then consuming the electric energy through the connection resistance to achieve braking. Since there is no physical contact, electric braking is very low cost and is the first choice of braking method. However, electric braking isn't very effective on EMUs at very low and high speeds. Air braking uses compressed air as a power source to push a friction block against the brake disc to achieve braking. But because of the physical contact, the cost is higher, due to increased wear and tear. Modern EMUs usually use electro-pneumatic braking as shown in Fig.1.39.

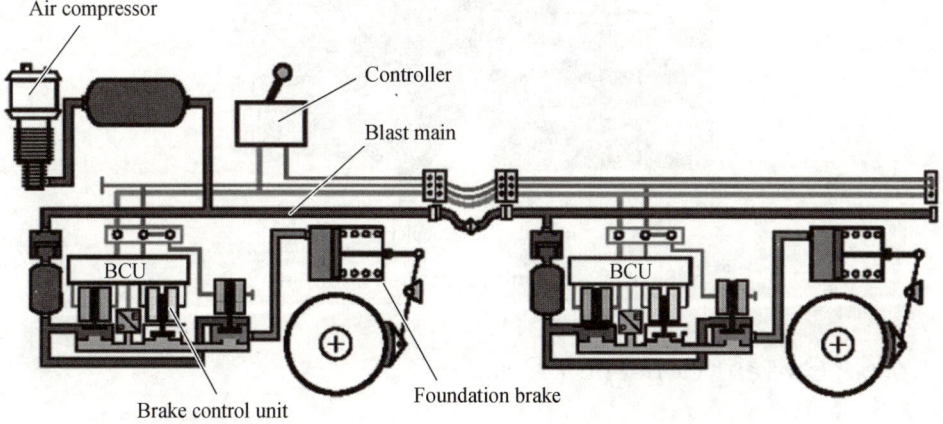

Fig.1.39 Electro-Pneumatic Braking

1.4.5 End Connection Device

The end connection device includes various coupler buffer devices, articulated devices and gangways, etc. The function of the end connection device is to couple cars, ease longitudinal impact, and transmit power and signals.

Generally, cars are organized into trains using couplers to connect each car as shown in Fig.1.40. However, articulated EMUs usually use articulated devices instead of couplers.

In order to improve the longitudinal stability of the EMUs, a buffer device is generally installed at the rear of the coupler to alleviate the impact of the EMUs. In addition, the electrical and air lines between the coaches must be well connected by means of simple and reliable connectors.

At the same time, in order to improve the sealing condition and air resistance of the train, it is necessary to adopt the use of inner and outer angways that are sealed and have a smooth transition on the outer surface.

Fig.1.40 Semi-permanent Coupler

1.4.6 Current Collection Device

The current collection device collects electric current and sends it to the traction motor.

Current collection devices can be divided into various types according to the current collecting method. High-speed trains usually use the pantograph as their current collection device, this is called upper current collection. Whereas subway trains use a third rail current collector this is called lower current collection. The pantograph can be raised and lowered as needed as shown in Fig.1.41.

In terms of the current collection device standard of high-speed trains all over the world some countries use a 1500 V DC power supply (such as Japan, Malaysia, etc.), some countries use a 3000 V DC power supply (such as: Italy, Spain, etc.), other countries use a low-frequency AC power supply (such as: Germany, Switzerland, etc.) and some countries use a industrial frequency AC power supply (such as: France, the United Kingdom, etc). All passenger dedicated lines in China use 50 Hz, 25 kV single-phase AC power supply.

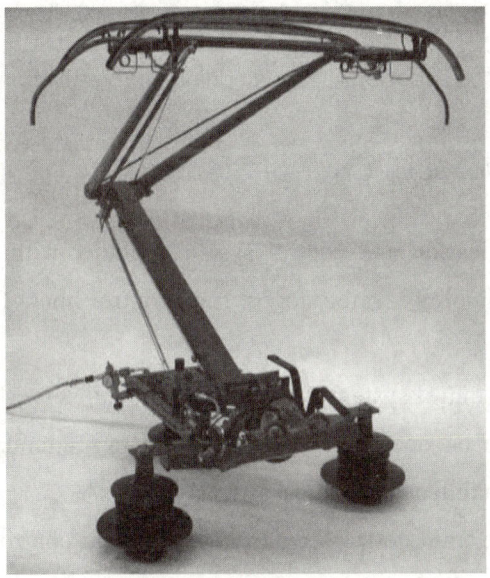

Fig.1.41 Pantograph

1.4.7 Interior Equipment

The function of interior equipment is to ensure the safety and comfort of passengers and the normal operation of the main equipment. Interior equipment includes fixtures in the car body for passengers and auxiliary equipment for EMUs operation.

The fixtures in the car body include: electricity, ventilation, heating, air conditioning, seats and handles, and passenger information systems.

Auxiliary equipment serving EMUs operation includes: battery box, relay box, main control box, air compressor, main air cylinder, auxiliary power supply device, various electrical switches and contactors, etc.

Layout of Air Conditioning and Ventilation System is shown in Fig.1.42.

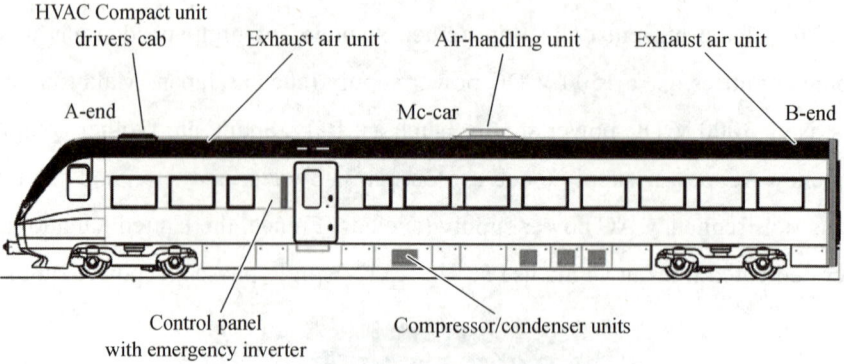

Fig.1.42　Layout of Air Conditioning and Ventilation System

1.4.8　Train Network Control System

The train communication and control system together with the subsystems and the conventional circuit technology (safety loops, train control lines) form the overall network train control system.

The train network control system is like the "brain and nerves" of the high speed train. It can provide guidance on operation to drivers and train attendants, as well as provide support for equipment maintenance and passenger services.

The function of the train network control system is to control, monitor and diagnose the traction, braking and all other equipment on the train.

The main components of the train network control system are the central control unit module, gateway module, input and output module, event recording module, repeater module, Ethernet switch module and human-computer interaction display module.

Homework

1. What are the classification methods of EMUs? Please briefly describe each.
2. How many technology platforms can China's existing EMUs be divided into?

3. Please briefly describe the meaning of the model and technical configuration code of Chinese standard EMUs.

4. What is a power decentralized EMUs?

5. Briefly describe the meaning of the EMUs name of the CR300BF-3006.

6. What are the components of an EMUs?

Chapter 2

EMUs Maintenance

Learning objectives

- Know the EMUs maintenance thought;
- Understand EMUs workshop and depot;
- Familiar with EMUs maintenance procedures and systems.
- Familiar with EMUs maintenance tools.

2.1 EMUs Maintenance Procedures and Systems

The maintenance of EMUs is an important part of railway transportation. The quality of EMUs maintenance directly relates to the safety of passengers' lives and property and to the economic benefits of enterprise. The essential tasks of EMUs maintenance include repair and maintenance and focusing on fault prevention. It also involves improving the maintenance management system and providing high-quality EMUs.

The maintenance of EMUs is mainly based on kilometers clocked (the distance of travel is subject to the management information system of the EMUs) and the operation time is supplemental. The standard procedure for EMUs maintenance is mainly to replace faulty parts. Faulty parts are gathered at EMUs depots where technicians figure out the fault and repair components.

EMUs maintenance adopts a system of planned preventive maintenance, which is divided into five levels of maintenance. Level Ⅰ and Ⅱ maintenance is operation maintenance, which is carried out at an EMUs Workshop. Level Ⅲ, Ⅳ and level Ⅴ maintenance is advanced maintenance, which is carried out at an EMUs depot and the manufacturer.

2.1.1 Level I Maintenance

Level Ⅰ maintenance refers to the regular (every 2-4 days) maintenance operation of an EMUs. This operation consists of a rapid routine inspection, testing and fault repair of the EMUs roof, undercarriage, sides and inside the vehicle and cab of the EMUs. Level Ⅰ maintenance operations take about 2 hours in an EMUs workshop and are carried out after service hours (usually at midnight).

The Level Ⅰ maintenance of EMUs is an integrated operation covering multiple professions and types of work. It is characterized by its rapidity and flowability. Level Ⅰ maintenance of EMUs is mainly undertaken by a Level Ⅰ maintenance team, assisted by other cooperative teams.

The Level Ⅰ maintenance team is mainly responsible for checking the Level Ⅰ maintenance scope of EMUs. Maintenance of short marshalling EMUs (8 Marshalling) is undertaken by one team and long marshalling EMUs (16 and 17 marshalling) require two teams.

Level Ⅰ maintenance teams are generally divided into an upper crew and lower crew according to the part of the EMUs they work on. The upper crew is mainly responsible for the relevant performance testing of the roof and cab of the EMUs. The lower crew is mainly responsible for the inspection of the underbody and both sides of the body and the interior of the EMUs.

According to the requirements of maintenance organization and management, in the EMUs depot tasks are divided into specific numbers No.1, No.2, No.3 and No.4. Operators are assigned a number and they then carry out those tasks and only referred to by the number they were assigned.

Fig.2.1 Upper Crew

Fig.2.2 Lower Crew

Other cooperative teams are mainly responsible for organization tasks outside the scope of the Level Ⅰ maintenance team, including the clearance of the access inspection garage, shuttle operation, catenary power supply operation, fault disposal, suction, cleaning operation and inspection and testing of on-board electrical equipment by the electrical department.

The Level I maintenance of EMUs can adopt the mode of non-electric (external power supply can be connected) - electric or electric - non-electric - electric operation.

2.1.2 Level II Maintenance

Level II maintenance refers to the periodic maintenance, inspection, testing and fault repair of all systems and components of an EMUs. This period is based on an EMUs clocked kilometers or time in operation. Compared with the rapid maintenance mode of level I maintenance, level II maintenance focuses on the in-depth maintenance of components and the troubleshooting of complex faults. This operation, carried out in an EMUs workshop, takes a long time and is generally undertaken during the day.

From the study of the EMUs system reliability and lifecycle, it is known that as the clocked kilometers of an EMUs accumulates, its components will suffer from wear and tear to varying degrees and the technical performance of said components will decline, which will affect the operation safety and comfort of EMUs. Maintenance measures such as inspection, lubrication and cleaning should be carried out routinely to lengthen the systems and service life of EMUs and to ensure components are maintained in good technical condition. For this reason, the concept of Level II maintenance is introduced between Level I maintenance and advanced maintenance.

Level II maintenance is the maintenance of all systems and components of an EMUs, standard Level II maintenance involves numerous tasks, which are time consuming and require work to be carried out all over the EMUs. At this stage, Level II maintenance of EMUs mainly adopts the method of project packaging and creating a maintenance framework. First, the maintenance cards for each system and component are developed, which are called maintenance items. Then, according to the system, component mechanism and maintenance depth requirements (there may be multiple maintenance cards for the same system and component with different maintenance depths), the running kilometer interval or time period is indicated in each maintenance card. Then, the similar items are packed together for repair, forming the level II maintenance.

The level II maintenance plan of EMUs consists of monthly plan, weekly plan and daily plan. The monthly plan is prepared by the EMUs depot and the weekly and daily plans are prepared and implemented by the EMUs workshop.

Level II maintenance of EMUs is carried out by a level II maintenance team and wheel axle team, the wheel axle team is mainly responsible for hollow axle ultrasonic testing, rim spoke ultrasonic testing and wheel tread modification. The level Ⅱ maintenance team is responsible for the level Ⅱ maintenance projects except those carried out by the wheel axle team. The EMUs workshop schedules the shifts of the wheel axle team and level Ⅱ maintenance team according to their working hours and the workload of the EMUs workshop. Coupler inspection testing is shown in Fig.2.3. Hollow axle ultrasonic testing is shown in Fig.2.4.

Fig.2.3　Coupler Inspection

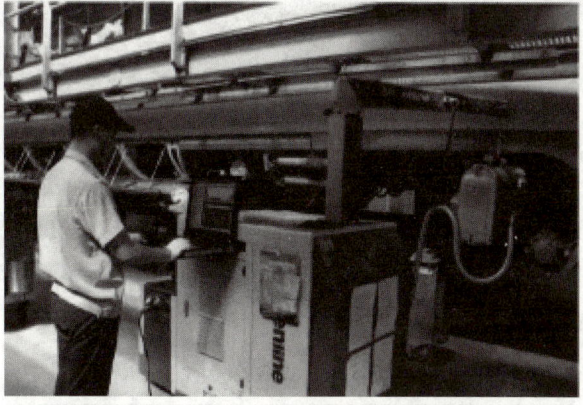

Fig.2.4　Hollow Axle Ultrasonic Testing

2.1.3　EMUs Advanced Maintenance

Level Ⅲ maintenance refers to the removal, disassembly, inspection, repair and testing of the EMUs bogies. Level Ⅲ maintenance also includes the disassembly and repair of the wheel set bearing and electric traction motors. This level of maintenance requires the use of special equipment so it is undertaken at an EMUs depot. It can be a lengthy process.

Level IV maintenance (Fig.2.5) refers to the disassembly and overhaul of an EMUs main systems. The EMUs bogies shall be dismantled completely and the traction motor, auxiliary motor, transmission gear and gearbox, main transformer, etc. shall be dismantled and inspected completely. All shafts and wheel groups shall be ultrasonic inspected and the pantograph, etc. shall be dismantled and repaired completely. The maintenance of some of the systems can be performed at an EMUs depot whilst many systems require maintenance at the manufacturer. After said maintenance is performed each main system is tested and the carriage body is painted if necessary. The EMUs is then ready to return to service.

Fig.2.5　EMUs Level IV Maintenance

Level V maintenance refers to the most advanced maintenance carried out on an EMUs. The whole EMUs is disassembled, most of the parts are replaced and the car body is painted. This level of maintenance usually takes place at the manufacturer.

Maintenance Cycle of EMUs is shown in Tab.2.1.

Tab.2.1　Maintenance Cycle of EMUs

	Level I	Level II	Level III	Level IV	Level V
CRH1	4000 km or 48 h	15 days	1 200 000 km	2 400 000 km	4 800 000 km
CHR2	4000 km or 48 h	30 000 km or 30 days	450 000 km or 1 year	900 000 km or 3 years	1 800 000 km or 6 years
CHR3	4000 km or 48 h	20 000 km	1 200 000 km	2 400 000 km	4 800 000 km
CHR5	4000 km or 48 h	60 000 km	1 200 000 km	2 400 000 km	4 800 000 km
CR400AF	4000 km or 48 h	20 000 km	1 200 000 km	2 400 000 km	4 800 000 km

2.2 EMUs Maintenance Site

2.2.1 EMUs Depots

The composition of EMUs depot generally includes: main line, operation maintenance shed, advanced maintenance shed and service facilities for depot staff. The main line includes entry lines exit lines and parking lines. The operation maintenance shed is the area where level Ⅰ maintenance and level Ⅱ maintenance is carried out and the temporary repair of EMUs. The advanced maintenance shed is used to undertake level Ⅲ, level Ⅳ maintenance and level Ⅴ maintenance of EMUs.

There are two general types of layout of an EMUs depots main line, operation maintenance shed, advanced maintenance shed. They are parallel and longitudinal. The advantages of the parallel layout is that it is compact and tidy and is a concentrated operation, while the disadvantages are that it requires a wide area and it is difficult to arrange the train washing line and testing line; the longitudinal layout is mainly applicable to long and narrow terrain. This layout has clear zoning, smooth train running and is easier to arrange the train washing line and testing line. The disadvantage is that the number of running lines is large and inconvenient for management. In practice the above two types of layout are rarely used alone but are used in combination.

Due to geography and practicalities, most EMUs depots are arranged in longitudinal end. Guangzhou EMUs depot is a typical example of longitudinal end layout, as shown in Fig.2.6. The parking lines and operation maintenance shed are arranged in longitudinal, and the operation maintenance shed and the advanced maintenance shed are arranged in parallel. The long and narrow landform is fully used, the zoning is clear, and the train runs smoothly, but the number of running lines is large.

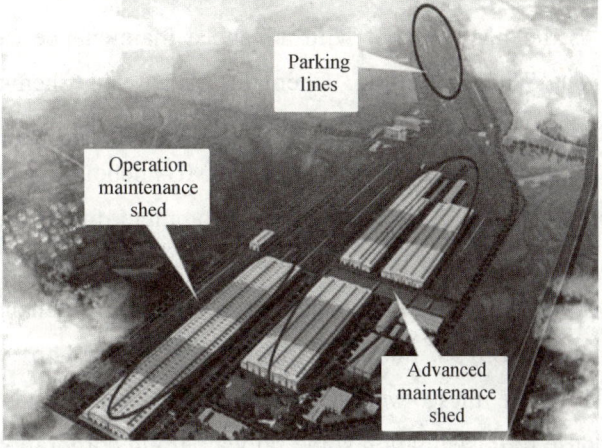

Fig.2.6　Layout of Guangzhou EMUs Depot

2.2.2　Classification and Location of EMUs Depots

By the end of 2020, China State Railway Group Co., Ltd had constructed 25 EMUs depots. Their distribution across China is shown in Fig.2.7.

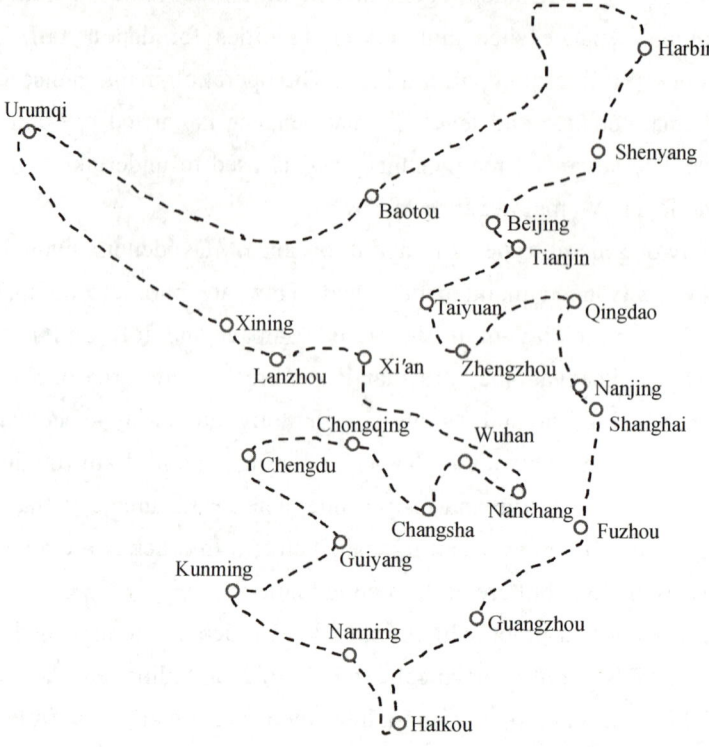

Fig.2.7　Location of EMUs Depots

EMUs depots can be roughly divided into three types according to the capacity and scope of maintenance.

The first type is the EMUs depot with advanced maintenance capacity, such as the Shanghai, Guangzhou, Wuhan, Beijing, Chengdu, Xi'an and Shenyang EMUs depots. These seven EMUs depots concentrate on different EMUs models and some of them have level Ⅲ, Ⅳ and Ⅴ maintenance capacity. These EMUs depots were built earlier and are located in transportation hub cities. They have complete functional departments and undertake more maintenance tasks.

The second type is the EMUs depot without advanced maintenance capacity. Due to the increasing number of EMUs, more and more EMUs workshops were being used to maintain EMUs. However these workshops don't have advanced level maintenance capabilities. In response to this situation some railway group corporations have constructed more EMUs depots, but have no plans to establish advanced maintenance capabilities. For professional centralized management, separate EMUs depots are established to facilitate management. These EMUs depots are indistinguishable from the first type except that they have no advanced maintenance capabilities. They also have their own independent department and EMUs. These type of depots can be found in Nanjing, Qingdao, Fuzhou and Harbin.

The third type of depot is a normal speed passenger train depot with an EMUs workshop. These depots are used for EMUs maintenance because some railway group corporations only have a few EMUs workshops or even only one. This type of EMUs workshop managed by normal passenger train depots have different function settings to those of other EMUs workshops. This kind of EMUs workshop has neither an advanced maintenance shed nor the opportunity to form an EMUs depot independently. These type of depots can be found in Nanning, Nanchang, Guiyang, Urumqi, Changsha and Haikou.

2.2.3　EMUs workshops

The EMUs workshop (Fig.2.7) is the place where daily EMUs maintenance operations are carried out, they are subordinate to EMUs depots. EMUs workshops are located at passenger transportation centers on the railway network e.g. Beijing. They are also found on lines with large passenger flow e.g. Beijing to Shanghai, in order to meet the technical requirements of rapid maintenance, safe, reliable and efficient operation. In principle, the inspection warehouse of the newly built EMUs workshop shall not be less than 6 railway lines and 12 standard group (8 Marshalling as a standard group). The capacity of the parking line and the temporary repair shed shall match the capacity of the inspection warehouse; the capacity of the washing garage (line) and the inspection line shall be able to handle the intensive preparation and testing of EMUs. The EMUs workshop needs to be equipped with complete relevant equipment, facilities and tooling according to the actual situation of maintenance. The infrastructure office of the EMUs workshop shall ensure that the construction and maintenance, investment in equipment and facilities of the EMUs workshop meet the operation and maintenance needs of EMUs. The facility and equipment management office of the EMUs workshop shall standardize the management, use, maintenance and repair of equipment and facilities and keep them in good technical condition. The establishment and cancellation of the EMUs workshops shall be approved by China State Railway Group Co., Ltd.

Fig.2.7 EMUs Workshop

2.2.4 EMUs Maintenance Team

EMUs maintenance implements the director responsibility system. The operation and maintenance of an EMUs requires 7-8 staff in order to maintain it. They consist of: a management team which is generally composed of workshop management personnel, technicians, scheduling staff and quality inspectors.

The main tasks of the management personnel include operation management, labor quota, bonus distribution, post star rating, attendance management, material purchase, accounting analysis, implementation of dual prevention mechanism, safety problem investigation, problem management and control, internal protection and fire protection, education and training, standardization, and team construction. The personnel are simplified, and the functions are set according to the actual needs of production, or set together with the technicians.

The main tasks of technicians include setting regulations (regulation interpretation, training, and organization of regulations), EMUs operation (train graph adjusting, shunting, crew standard management), maintenance (level I and level II maintenance standards, temporary repair standards, technical changes, renovations, remediation), axles (wheel-set flaw detection of EMUs, maintenance process, fault management), equipment (management, use, maintenance and repair, construction operations, information system management), diagnosis (EMUs troubleshooting, Analysis, disposal, prevention and control).

The main tasks of scheduling staff include level Ⅰ and level Ⅱ maintenance plans for EMUs, organizing production, monitoring, and assistance.

The main tasks of quality inspectors are EMUs quality process control and result confirmation; implementation of EMUs maintenance quality inspection methods, inspection scope, and work requirements. The quality standards of the EMUs operating on the railway shall not be lower than the "Regulations on the Quality Standards for departure from the workshops of EMUs". When entrusting maintenance, it should meet the requirements of the maintenance rules of China State Railway Group Co., Ltd. The quality inspectors are required to check the quality of level Ⅰ maintenance operations, and confirm that key faults have been fixed. They also inspect the quality of level Ⅱ maintenance operations, according to the importance of the project, confirm the operation process, important nodes or results, etc. Check the quality of temporary repair work. Joint inspection of the EMUs workshop. EMUs use quality appraisal. Technical change quality supervision.

A production team which routinely sets up maintenance crews (level Ⅰ and level Ⅱ maintenance crews), temporary maintenance crews, and other direct production teams and crew.

The maintenance crews are responsible for level Ⅰ and level Ⅱ maintenance, testing and troubleshooting of EMUs, preparation of EMUs, operation and daily maintenance of the EMUs maintenance equipment and dealing with the key faults or entrusted maintenance items found by the on-board mechanic of the EMUs that affect the operation safety of the EMUs. They are also responsible for the quality and safety within the scope of maintenance. They are subdivided into level Ⅰ maintenance crews and level Ⅱ maintenance crews. The level Ⅰ maintenance crews can be compiled into a specific maintenance crew according to different model of EMUs.

The level Ⅱ maintenance crews can be subdivided into an item maintenance crew and a special maintenance crew. The item maintenance crews are responsible for the implementation of the level Ⅱ maintenance work package item and the repairing of faults. The special maintenance crews are responsible for professional maintenance of air conditioners and exterior doors, as well as the implementation of seasonal key projects and waste utilization projects. Depending on the situation, it can be further evolved into an M maintenance crew, an air conditioning crew, and a rectification crew.

The main work of the temporary repair crews is the replacement of large components such as wheel sets, repairing wheels, large-scale temporary repairs and technical transformation.

The crew is responsible for managing the on-board EMUs mechanics, operating EMUs equipment, monitoring EMUs operation and the technical status of the equipment, correctly judging and properly handling EMUs equipment failures, handling relevant handovers, and undertaking some driving functions. According to the division of labor of the line, the crew can be expanded to multiple crews, or even the crew work combination of the EMUs, and an independent crew workshop can be established.

The EMUs team is also equipped with flaw detection crews, equipment crews as well as material crews and internal quality control crews.

The flaw detection crew is responsible for the flaw detection of the hollow shaft; the equipment team is responsible for the "management, use, maintenance and repair" of equipment and facilities, construction cooperation, tool management and file management. The material crew is responsible for the management of the materials and accessories of the EMUs. The internal quality control crew is mainly responsible for video monitoring and operation evaluation in the EMUs workshop.

2.3 EMUs Maintenance Tools

There are many kinds of EMUs tools. This section only introduces the general maintenance tools. All EMUs workshops implement centralized and unified management of the maintenance tools and measuring instruments of EMUs and measuring instruments must be used within their valid period of verification. The on-board train tools and measuring instruments of EMUs follow the principle of "tools belong to the EMUs, not to the train crews". The on-board train tools are usually stored in the EMUs tool room. When using tools and measuring instruments, the mechanic on the EMUs shall take good care of public property, use them correctly according to their functions and requirements, not use them roughly and indiscriminately and put them back their in place after use. Personal and public tools and measuring instruments should be carefully maintained and used correctly, especially precision instruments such as measuring instruments which should be oiled regularly to prevent rust. Measuring instruments should not be used under any of the following circumstances:

① No identification certificate or calibration certificate.
② Exceed the verification and calibration period.
③ Unqualified after inspection.
④ Non-legal unit of measurement verification.
⑤ The use of which is expressly prohibited by the state

The common maintenance tools used on EMUs include: screwdriver, pliers, wrench, on-train tool kit and measuring tools. Types of Screwdriver are shown in Tab.2.2.

Tab.2.2 Types of Screwdriver

Name	Specification		Picture
Slotted screwdriver	Description	Used to turn a screw to force it into place, usually has a thin wedge-shaped head that fits into a slot or notch in the head of the screw	
	Instruction	① Insert the thin wedge head into the slot or notch of the screw head; ② Turn clockwise or counterclockwise to secure or loosen the screw	
	Notes/Warning	① When used for electrical wiring, live operation is strictly prohibited; ② Pay attention to the specifications, do not use it as a chisel or rod; ③ Wipe off the oil of the thin wedge tip before use	
Phillips screwdriver	Description	Used to turn a screw to force it into place, usually has a thin wedge-shaped head that fits into a slot or notch in the head of the screw	
	Instruction	① Insert the thin wedge head into the slot or notch of the screw head; ② Turn clockwise or counterclockwise to secure or loosen the screw	
	Notes/Warning	① When used for electrical wiring, live operation is strictly prohibited; ② Pay attention to the specifications, do not use it as a chisel or rod; ③ Wipe off the oil of the thin wedge tip before use	
Screwdriver set	Description	The screwdriver set contains a variety of wedge-shaped heads such as a slotted, a phillips, and a torx. Used to turn a screw to force it into place, with thin wedge-shaped heads on both ends that fit into slots or notches corresponding to the head of the screw	
	Instruction	① Insert the thin wedge head into the slot or notch of the screw head; ② Turn clockwise or counterclockwise to secure or loosen the screw	
	Notes/Warning	① When used for electrical wiring, live operation is strictly prohibited; ② Pay attention to the specifications, do not use it as a chisel or rod; ③ Wipe off the oil of the thin wedge tip before use	

Types of pliers are shown in Tab.2.3.

Tab.2.3   Types of Pliers

Name	Specification		Picture
Needle-nose pliers	Description	Needle-nose pliers are mainly used to cut single-strand and multi-strand wires with thin wire diameters. And crimp single-strand wire splices and strip plastic insulation. It can be used in tight work spaces	
	Instruction	Generally operated with the right hand, hold the two handles of the needle-nose pliers to start clamping or cutting work	
	Notes/Warning	When using, be careful not to point the cutting edge towards yourself, and put it back in place after use	
Diagonal pliers	Description	Diagonal pliers are mainly used to cut wires, excess leads of components, and are also often used to cut insulating sleeves, nylon cable ties, etc. instead of general scissors	
	Instruction	Hold the grip of the diagonal pliers with your thumb and four other right fingers, with the blade of the diagonal pliers forward, and forcefully cut through the target	
	Notes/Warning	① Before use, check whether the insulation of the insulating handle is in good condition; ② When cutting the live wire, the phase line and the neutral line cannot be cut at the same time; ③ The insulating tube of the clamp handle should be replaced in time after damage, and it should not be used reluctantly to prevent accidents from touching the live parts during operation	
Wire pliers	Description	Wire pliers are used to bend and twist cylindrical metal parts and cut wires, and their cutting edges can also be used to cut fine wires	
	Instruction	It is generally operated with the right hand, and the knife edge of the pliers is facing inward, that is, toward the operator, so as to control the cutting part. Then use your little finger to stretch between the two pliers handles to press against the pliers handles, and open the pliers head, so that it is more flexible to separate the pliers handles	

Continue

Name	Specification		Picture
Wire pliers	Notes/Warning	① Before use, check whether the insulation of the insulating handle is in good condition; ② When cutting the live wire, the phase line and the neutral line cannot be cut at the same time; ③ The insulating tube of the clamp handle should be replaced in time after damage, and it should not be used reluctantly to prevent accidents from touching the live parts during operation	
90-degree angled internal circlip pliers	Description	The 90-degree angled internal circlip pliers are special tools used to remove or install the positioning circlips that are clamped between the holes or on the shaft to prevent the axial movement of the parts	
	Instruction	Insert the pliers into the two holes of the circlip, and then expand or reduce the inner diameter	
	Notes/Warning	① The force should be stable to prevent falling off or breaking; ② Wear gloves to prevent injury after the circlip breaks; ③ Wear protective glasses	

Types of wrend are shown in Tab.2.4.

Tab.2.4　Types of Wrench

Name	Specification		Picture
Adjustable wrench	Description	An adjustable wrench is a tool used to tighten and loosen nuts and bolts of different sizes	
	Instruction	① When in use, adjust the size of the wrench according to the parts to be screwed; ② Make the opening line of the wrench parallel to the hexagon of the nut; ③ Screw the nut evenly in the correct direction to make the fixed jaw subject to the main force	
	Notes/Warning	① When turning large nuts, a large torque is usually used and the hand should be held at the end of the handle; ② When turning small nuts, the torque used is not large, but the nuts are too small to slip easily, so the hand should be held close to the plate head. ③ The adjustable wrench cannot be reversed to avoid damage to the plate lip, and the steel pipe cannot be used to extend the handle to increase the torque	

Continue

Name	Specification		Picture
Double offset ring spanner	Description	Double offset ring spanner is used in supplementary tightening and similar operations where a large torque can be applied to a bolt or nut using a double offset ring spanner	
	Instruction	When using the double offset ring spanner, push the connection between the double offset ring spanner and the bolt with the left hand, keep the double offset ring spanner fully matched with the bolt to prevent slipping, and hold the other end of the double offset ring spanner with the right hand and apply force. The double offset ring spanner can completely surround the heads of the bolts and nuts, so the corners of the bolts will not be damaged, and a large torque can be applied	
	Notes/ Warning	① When turning, it is strictly forbidden to put the extended pipe on the wrench to extend the length of the wrench to increase the torque, and it is strictly forbidden to hit the wrench to increase the torque, otherwise the tool will be damaged; ② It is strictly forbidden to use a double offset ring spanner with cracks and serious wear on the inner hole	
Static combination wrench	Description	A static combination wrench is a tool used to tighten and loosen nuts	
	Instruction	① Select the corresponding wrench according to the characteristics of the fasteners; ② Hold the end of the wrench handle by hand, tighten it clockwise and loosen it counterclockwise	
	Notes/ Warning	When using the wrench, keep the offset ring spanner fully engaged with the bolt to prevent slipping	
Double box end ratcheting wrench	Description	Double box end ratcheting wrench is a manual screw tightening tool that is used to fasten or loosen a bolt or nut in a narrow or hard-to-access position	
	Instruction	First select the appropriate size ratchet according to the bolt or nut to be rotated, then select the appropriate direction ratchet according to the direction of rotation or adjust the direction of the two-way ratchet, and finally put the ratchet around the bolt or nut and rotate	

Continue

Name		Specification	Picture
Double box end ratcheting wrench	Notes/ Warning	① Adjust the correct ratchet direction before use; ② Choose a suitable combination; ③ The tightening torque should not be too large. Make sure that the ratchet wheel and the bolt or nut are in complete agreement when using it; ④ In the process of using the sleeve, hold the connection between the handle and the sleeve with your left hand, and do not shake it, so as to prevent the sleeve from slipping out or damaging the edges and corners of the bolt and nut	
Hex Allen Key	Description	The Hex Allen key exerts force on the screw through torque, which greatly reduces the user's force	
	Instruction	Place the Hex Allen key in the hexagonal socket of the screw. Tighten the screws clockwise. Loosen the screw counterclockwise	
	Notes/ Warning	① When using the Hex Allen Key, it should be well matched with the screwed part before applying force. If the contact is not good, the force will easily slip off, causing the operator's body to be unbalanced; ② When using the locking wrench and Allen wrench, pay attention to selecting the appropriate specifications and models to prevent slipping and hurting your hands	
Torque wrench	Description	When screw and bolt tightness is critical, using a torque wrench allows the operator to apply a specific torque value	
	Instruction	① Set the desired torque value and turn the locking device to the lock position. Adjust the torque from a small value to a large value. If it exceeds the set value, adjust it back to a value lower than the set torque value; ② The application of force should be steady and slow, to avoid impact and sound (that is, after the spring is released), the application of force must be stopped.	
	Notes/ Warning	① Do not directly adjust from the maximum value to the minimum value; ② Check the fit of the torque wrench driver before use; ③ After use, the set value needs to be adjusted back to the minimum score; ④ Do not try to overload	

Continue

Name	Specification		Picture
Electric wrench	Description	Electric wrench is a rechargeable portable torque tool	
	Instruction	Select a sleeve of appropriate size and install it at the joint. The torque can be adjusted at the rear end of the joint. Hold the handle of the electric drill tightly and hook the start button with the index finger. There is a steering switch on the upper part of the start button, which can be selected according to the actual operation requirements. Tighten or loosen the bolts	
	Notes/Warning	It is strictly forbidden to use the wrench over the torque value	

Types of on-train tool kit are shown as in Tab.2.5.

Tab.2.5 On-train tool kit

Name	Specification		Picture
Flashlight with Video Camera	Description	The flashlight with video camera is used for lighting and audio-visual recording during the maintenance process of the EMUs	
	Instruction	① Turn on the flashlight with video camera; ② Set the worker number; ③ Set the operation ENU number; ④ Setting process; ⑤ Press the camera/photo button to record video or take photos	
	Notes/Warning	It is strictly forbidden to use the flashlight with video camera as a percussion tool	
Four corner key	Description	The four corner key is used to open the lock of corresponding components in the EMUs	
	Instruction	Insert the four corner holes into the lock cylinder and turn it clockwise or counterclockwise to achieve the switch lock effect	
	Notes/Warning	The key and lock should correspond	
Signal flags	Description	The railway signal flags are used to convey information about the operating conditions of the train the status of the running equipment, and the instructions and commands of the train to the railway operators through the color and method of the signal flag	

Continue

Name	Specification		Picture
Signal flags	Instruction	① Stop signal: unfolded red signal flag; ② Deceleration signal: The unfolded yellow signal flag; ③ The signal to direct the train to the direction of the guide: the unfolded green signal flag shakes left and right at the lower part; ④ The signal to direct the train to go in the opposite direction of the guide: the red signal flag that is folded is held upright and horizontal, and then the green signal flag that is unfolded is used to move up and down	
	Notes/Warning	When there is no yellow signal flag, press the green signal flag several times to indicate the deceleration signal	
Handheld signal lights	Description	Handheld signal lights are suitable for watchmen, shunters, train captains, and various construction sites that need to display signals	
	Instruction	① According to different models, the handheld signal lights can be divided into: "red-green-white three" colors and "red-yellow-white three" colors ② When using, according to different working environments and needs, select the corresponding color to meet the signal requirements to be guided and indicated	
	Notes/Warning	When using it, make sure that the color range selected by the hand-held signal light is consistent with the actual color displayed to prevent display errors caused by equipment failures	
Wheel chock	Description	The wheel chock stopper is a device to prevent slippage when the EMUs has no parking brake device or when there is no power to stop on a straight road	
	Instruction	When setting the wheel chock, it should be close to the wheel, and one wheel chock should be installed at the front and rear of the one-side wheel of the first axle of the head car	
	Notes/Warning	When the wheel chock is removed, it must be confirmed that the EMUs is in the brake application state	

Continue

Name	Specification		Picture
Stop blocks	Description	When the stop blocks are used for the EMUs to stop or park on the ramp, the stop blocks can be used to prevent slipping	
	Instruction	When the stop block is set, the tip is facing uphill and close to the wheel tread, and the bottom is parallel to the rail. ① For 8-car EMUs that do not have the parking brake function or the parking brake function is abnormal, when parking on the slope, set 6 stop blocks from the bottom end of the slope to the upward direction, one for each axle, and set them to the left and right; ② When parking the 8-car group EMUs with normal braking function, when parking on a slope below 20‰, no stop block is required; when parking on a slope of 20‰ and above, set 2 stop blocks from the bottom of the slope to the uphill direction, 1 for each axis, set crosswise on the left and right sides	
	Notes/Warning	After the EMUs stop block is set, make sure that the wheels compact the stop block	
Infrared thermometers	Description	Infrared thermometers are used to measure the temperature of non-contact objects	
	Instruction	To measure an object, point the lens directly at the object to be measured and press and hold the switch to measure. The SCAN symbol appears on the screen, indicating that the temperature is being measured. Release the switch, the HOLD symbol will appear on the screen, indicating that the actual temperature of the measured object is displayed on the screen	
	Notes/Warning	Choose the appropriate measurement distance	

Types of measuring tools are shown in Tab.2.6.

Tab.2.6　Types of Measuring tools

Name	Specification		Picture
Feeler gauge	Description	A feeler gauge is a measuring tool mainly used for the measurement of gap spacing. A feeler gauge is a gauge composed of a set of thin steel sheets with different thickness levels	
	Instruction	① Insert the feeler gauge into the measured gap, and pull the feeler gauge back and forth. If you feel a little resistance, it means that the gap value is close to the value marked on the feeler gauge. If the resistance is too large or too small when pulling, it means that the gap value is smaller or larger than the value marked on the feeler gauge; ② When measuring and adjusting the gap, first select a feeler gauge that meets the gap requirements and insert it into the measured gap. Then while adjusting, pull the feeler gauge until you feel a little resistance and tighten the lock nut. At this time, the value marked by the feeler gauge is the measured gap value	
	Notes/ Warning	It is not allowed to bend the feeler gauge violently during the measurement process, or insert the feeler gauge into the detected gap with greater force	
Dynamometer	Description	The small tensile force meter has the advantages of high precision, easy operation and portability, and has a peak switching operation knob, which can display the peak load value and the continuous load value	
	Instruction	① Correctly estimate the tension range, and select a tension meter within the range; ② Hook the tension meter hook with the reliable part of the measured object; ③ Stretch along the direction of the force, and measure the actual tensile force	
	Notes/ Warning	It is strictly forbidden to use the tension meter over the range	

Continue

Name		Specification	Picture
Thread gauge	Description	Thread gauge is a tool for checking the condition of the inner hole thread	
	Instruction	① The "GO" end cannot be screwed in, which means that the pitch diameter of the thread is too large and the product is not qualified, but it can be qualified by reprocessing; ② The "NO GO" end passes, indicating that the pitch diameter is small, the product is unqualified, and it cannot be reworked; ③ The "GO" end can be rotated freely at any position of the thread, and the "NO GO" end can not be screwed after one to two or three turns (the head of the thread is not screwed out), indicating that the detected diameter of the external thread is just within "Within the tolerance zone", it is a qualified product	
	Notes/ Warning	The thread Gauge that has passed the quality inspection should be used, and the thread Gauge should be calibrated regularly with a calibration tool	
Spirit level	Description	A Spirit Level is a tool used to indicate how parallel (level) or perpendicular (plumb) a surface is relative to the earth	
	Instruction	① Place the spirit level on the surface of the object; ② Make sure the spirit tube runs parallel to the object. Allow the bubble to float to the top of the spirit tube. Put eyes at spirit level with the spirit tube. In order to get an accurate reading, close one eye; ③ Take note of where the bubble is inside the spirit tube. If it's centered between the lines on the tube, object is level. If the bubble is to the right of the lines, object slopes downward right-to-left. If the bubble is to the left of the lines, object slopes downward left-to-right	
	Notes/ Warning	When using the spirit level, observe that the appearance is not damaged, and the measurement surface of the spirit level is not bent otherwise there will be measurement errors	

Homework

1. How many levels can an EMUs maintenance be divided into? Describe the maintenance contents separately.
2. How to confirm whether the EMUs needs maintenance?
3. What are the locations for EMUs maintenance?
4. What are the EMUs depots for advanced maintenance?
5. What are the general tools for EMUs maintenance?

Chapter 3

EMUs Body Structure and Maintenance

Learning objectives

- Know the EMUs body structure design principles.
- Know the common materials of the EMUs body
- Familiar with EMUs body composition.
- Familiar with EMUs body maintenance.

3.1 EMUs Body Structure

3.1.1 EMUs Body Structure Design Principles

In high-speed train car body design the main design goals include aerodynamics, comfort, safety and a lightweight structure. However these goals are mutually restrictive. Therefore in order to achieve these goals the following requirements must be considered in the car body design of high-speed trains.

(1) Car body strength: in order to ensure that the EMUs has sufficient strength during operation, it must be able to withstand certain load conditions to meet the strength design specifications of the EMUs.

(2) Car body stiffness: it minimizes EMUs deformation and torsional angular displacement of the car body.

(3) The natural frequency of the car body: it is closely related to the running quality and safety of the EMUs. Therefore, the first bend mode frequency of the car body is limited to a certain extent in the specification.

(4) Collision-resistant safety protection of the car body: it is required to design a stronger passenger compartment structure, and at the same time, an energy absorption area

is set up in the non-passenger area of the car body to absorb kinetic energy from impacts and ensure the safety of passengers.

(5) Lightweight structure: on the premise of ensuring safety and service life, try to make the structure as lightweight as possible.

3.1.2 Materials of EMUs Car Body

The materials used in the manufacturing of high-speed train car bodies in China mainly include stainless steel, high-strength weathering steel and aluminum alloy.

1. Weathering steel

High weather resistant structural steel is a kind of steel with high atmospheric corrosion resistance. In the railway vehicle industry, it is usually referred to as "weathering steel". The research shows that the atmospheric corrosion resistance of weathering steel will be significantly improved if the content of Cu, P, Cr, Si and other elements is appropriate.

In the mid-1960s, China began to develop weathering steel. Through the large-scale research of major iron and steel enterprises, a type of weathering steel was developed using China's mineral resources. In particular, the research on the atmospheric corrosion resistance of carbon steel by rare earth elements from China's unique mineral resources made significant discoveries. The corrosion resistance of copper phosphorus weathering steel used in Chinese railway vehicles is generally about twice that of ordinary carbon steel, and the corrosion resistance of copper phosphorus chromium nickel weathering steel is 2–3 times that of ordinary carbon steel. The grades of weathering steel for railway vehicles in China include Q295GN11, Q295GNHIJ and Q345GNH.

2. Stainless steel

Stainless steel has excellent corrosion resistance and its lightweight is ideal for high-speed train car bodies. Due to the poor corrosion resistance of ordinary carbon steel, the car body structure is seriously corroded, which brings great difficulties to the design department. In order to prolong the service life of the vehicle, the section size has to be increased in the design, resulting in the increase of the body's own mass. Stainless steel has excellent corrosion resistance. On the premise of strength, stiffness and service performance, it can reduce the plate thickness and realize the lightweight of the car body. Compared with ordinary steel car body structures, car body structures made of stainless steel have a 10%–20% lower mass. The reduction of weight can reduce energy consumption and improve operation speed, which has significant economic benefits.

On the one hand, due to the good corrosion resistance, the car body does not need coating, and the car body made of stainless steel can reduce the manufacturing hours. On the other hand, the current vehicle maintenance work is mainly to repair the corrosion caused by ordinary steel vehicles, which accounts for most of the repair hours and seriously affects the turnover of vehicles. The stainless steel car body has excellent corrosion resistance and does not have the corrosion problem of ordinary steel vehicles. The daily maintenance work is mainly cleaning, which reduces the maintenance workload and improves the utilization rate of vehicles.

The stainless steel used to manufacture for car bodies include SUS304 and SUS301L. In short, low carbon austenitic stainless steel with good corrosion resistance, high yield limit, high fatigue strength and good welding processability shall be selected.

A low carbon austenitic stainless steel car body weighs 15% less than a weathering steel car body.

3. Aluminum alloy

The attempt to make car bodies from aluminum alloys began as early as the first half of the 20th century and was first used on subway and suburban trains, and later on ordinary trains. In the 1990s, train manufacturers began to make car bodies out of large hollow extruded aluminium alloy profiles.

Make aluminum alloy the leading material for high-speed train production. The advantages of aluminum alloy bodywork are as follows:

(1) The manufacturing process is simple and saves processing costs. Aluminum alloy has good plasticity and easy extrusion. According to the requirements of the optimal design of the car body structure, aluminum profiles with various complex shapes can be extruded, with a width of 600 – 800 mm and a length of 30 m. the welding workload is greatly reduced and the manufacturing process of the vehicle is simplified. The total manufacturing workload is about 40% less than that of the steel car body.

(2) Light weight. The car body assembled with large extruded aluminum profiles, because the profiles are thin-walled and hollow, and many transverse members are reduced, so that the mass of the aluminum alloy vehicle is greatly reduced. The mass ratio of steel car body, stainless steel car body and aluminum alloy car body reaches 10:7:5. In addition, the car body welded by large extruded aluminum profiles has high equivalent bending stiffness, and the stiffness can meet the design requirements.

(3) Good running quality. The aluminum alloy car body has a small self-weight, which can save traction power, improve acceleration performance, reduce braking power, and improve dynamic performance, and has good sealing and sound insulation performance, which improves comfort.

(4) Corrosion resistance, which can reduce maintenance costs. Aluminum alloy has good corrosion resistance, thus extending the service life of the EMUs and reducing the maintenance workload.

(5) The aluminum alloy body also has the advantages of smooth and beautiful appearance.

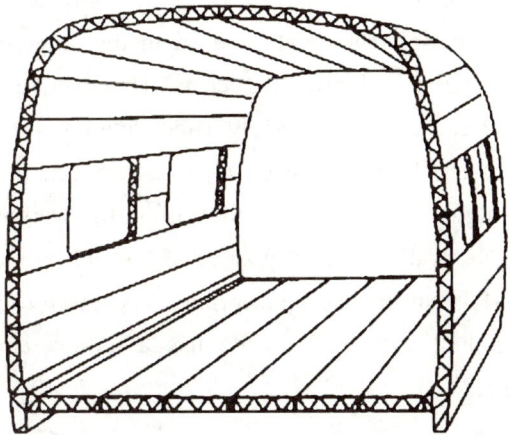

Fig.3.1　Welded car body structure of large hollow extruded aluminum profile

"Fuxing" series EMUs was put into operation in 2017 in China. Its car body is made of lightweight aluminum alloy. The thinnest aluminum alloy section is only 1.5 mm and the whole body is about 7 t. It is the lightest EMUs in the world. It has excellent energy-saving and environmental protection performance.

In order to further reduce the mass, improve the sound insulation performance, and improve the convenience of design and manufacture, some EMUs have begun to try the fiber-reinforced plastic sandwich structure instead of metal to manufacture the car body. Fiber-reinforced plastics have the advantages of light weight, high specific strength, high fatigue resistance, low crack growth rate, good structural damping, and good thermal insulation and corrosion resistance. The disadvantage is that the elastic modulus is low, the bending torsional stiffness is worse than that of metal, and the price is expensive. If the car body is made of carbon fiber, it will be 30% lighter than the aluminum alloy car body, which is an ideal material for the next generation of high-speed trains.

3.2　EMUs Body Composition

The car body of the EMUs is divided into two types: the head car body and the middle car body. The head car body is composed of the chassis, side walls, roof, end wall, body accessories and the head structure of the driver's cab. The middle car body is composed of the chassis, side walls, roof, end walls and body accessories.

The following takes the CRH2 EMUs as an example to introduce.

The CRH2 EMUs is mainly composed of hollow profiles to form a double-hulled car body structure. The double-shell structure is slightly heavier than the single-shell structure. However, the hollow profile has the characteristics of high section stiffness, which can remove the reinforcing material that must be used in the single-shell structure, thereby reducing the number of parts and reducing costs. However, excessive pursuit of the lightweight of high-speed EMUs will adversely affect ride comfort and train aerodynamic performance. Since more emphasis is placed on ride comfort, the body structure is not simply pursuing light weight, but reasonably controlling the weight of the body structure. Therefore, the roof and side walls of the high-speed EMUs all use a double-shell structure, and the weight of the EMUs car body is appropriately increased to improve the comfort of the EMUs. The double-shell structural profile has a hollow cavity, and the structure diagram is shown in Fig.3.2.

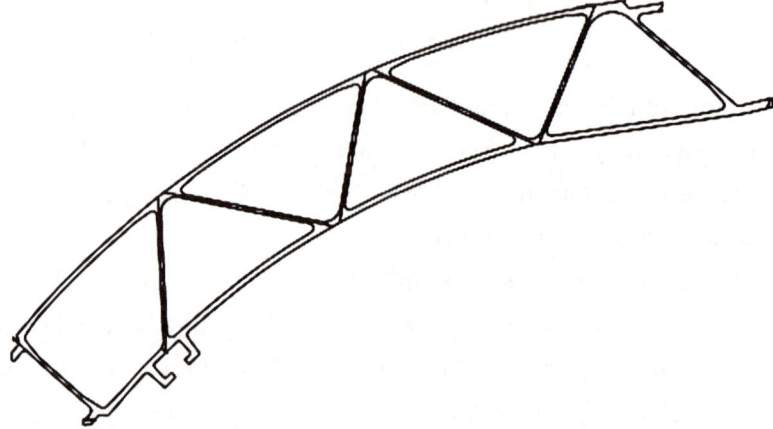

Fig.3.2 The Structure of Double-Shell Structural Profile

The car body of CRH2 EMUs is mainly composed of chassis, side wall, roof, end wall, under-vehicle equipment compartment, cowcatcher, etc. (the head car also includes the driver's cab).

3.2.1 Chassis

The chassis of the EMUs car body (Fig.3.3) mainly includes traction beams, sleeper beams, side beams, end beams, cross beams and corrugated floors. The side beams are made of aluminum alloy extruded profiles by tailor welding.

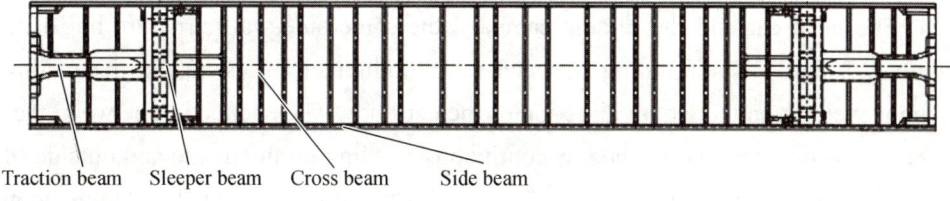

Traction beam   Sleeper beam   Cross beam   Side beam

Fig.3.3   The Chassis of Middle Car Body

The traction beam is mainly welded by aluminum alloy extruded profiles and aluminum alloy plates. It connects the end beam and the sleeper beam of the chassis of the EMUs car body, and provides corresponding additional structures for the coupler draft gears. The longitudinal load transmitted by the coupler draft gears acts on the traction beam through the coupler seat fixed on the traction beam, and then is transmitted to the entire EMUs car body structure through the structure such as the sleeper beam to realize the overall bearing. The coupler seat and the traction beam are connected by riveting, and the corresponding parts of the traction beam corresponding to the coupler draft gears are partially reinforced.

The sleeper beam is welded by aluminum alloy extruded profiles and aluminum plates to support the car body load. Corresponding structures are arranged on the corbel to ensure the normal connection with the bogie suspension system. At the center of sleeper beam, it is welded to the traction beam. There is a rescue support seat on the outside of the sleeper beam, which is convenient for jacking up the EMUs during rescue and maintenance.

Side beams refer to the longitudinal beams located on the left and right sides under the floor of the chassis, and are the key components for connecting the underframe and the side walls to form a EMUs car body. The side beam is not only the main part of the side wall, but also the main part of the chassis.

The end beams are welded by aluminum alloy extruded profiles and aluminum alloy plates.

The cross beam is made of aluminum alloy extruded profiles, located under the floor of the chassis, which plays the role of hanging equipment and balancing the load.

In order to adapt to the installation of the head structure of the driver's cab, the side beam part of the head chassis is adjusted correspondingly with respect to the chassis of middle car body.

3.2.2   Side Wall

The side wall of the EMUs body is made of large hollow extruded aluminum profiles, and there is no inner column. The cross-sectional view of the side wall structure is shown in

Fig.3.4. The head car and the middle car have the same side wall structure but different longitudinal lengths. The welding between the aluminum profiles adopts the method of continuous welding in the length direction of the car body. The connection between the side wall and the roof adopts the method of continuous welding on the inside and outside of the vehicle. The connection between the side wall and the side beam of the chassis adopts a segment welding structure on the inside of the EMUs, and the outside of the EMUs is a continuous welding method.

Long T-slots are reserved on the extruded aluminum profiles at the installation positions of the luggage rack, side top panel and side wall panel to facilitate the installation of interior components. In order to ensure the opening space of the side pull door, the doorway of the side wall is designed as an integrated box structure, as shown in Fig.3.5.

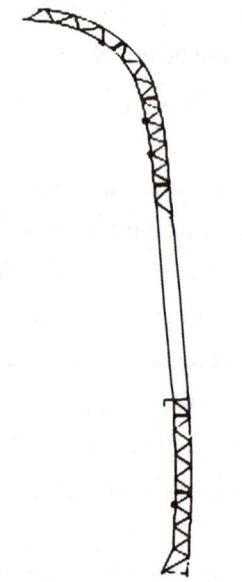

Fig.3.4 Structure Cross-Section of Side Wall

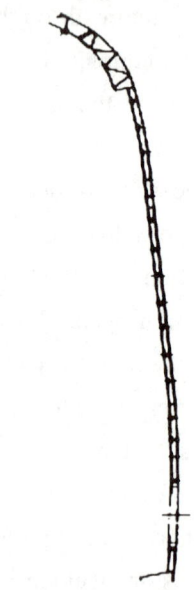

Fig.3.5 Structural Cross-Section of Side Wall Doorway

3.2.3 Roof

The roof is the upper structure of the EMUs car body, and is the installation basis for roof equipment such as pantographs and high-voltage cables.

The roof of the EMUs is composed of large hollow extruded profiles. The roof of the head car and the roof of the middle car have the same structure but different longitudinal lengths. The welding between the roof profiles adopts continuous welding in the length direction of the car body. The connection between the roof and the side walls adopts the continuous welding structure on the inside and outside of the vehicle. In addition, on the inside of the roof panel, sound and heat insulation materials are laid.

3.2.4 End Wall

One side of the head car body is designed with end walls, and both sides of the middle car are designed with end walls. According to the layout of the EMUs sanitary facilities, the end wall is mainly divided into two structural forms, namely split type and integral type. For EMUs with sanitary facilities at the ends, the end walls are of a split structure. The outer plate of the split structure is provided with an opening for transporting the glass fiber reinforced plastics module of the toilet. After the transportation is completed, the blocking plate welded by the aluminum plate and the aluminum profile skeleton group is installed with bolts, and the sealing material is filled to maintain air tightness. For EMUs without sanitary facilities at the ends, the end walls are of a Integral structure, which is a welded structure composed of aluminum plates and aluminum profile skeletons.

Both the split type and the integral type outer end wall are provided with a structure suitable for the installation of the gangway on the outer end frame, which can be quickly connected by bolts, which makes the installation of the gangway convenient and fast, and greatly reduces the construction time and labor intensity. In addition, there are boarding handrails on the end walls.

3.2.5 Driver's Cab

The driver's cab is the workplace where the driver obtains information, makes decisions, commands and controls related systems, and drives the train to complete various tasks. There is a driver's cab at each end of the EMUs. A partition door is installed on the partition wall between the driver's cab and the passenger compartment. A console and a driver's seat are arranged in the front center of the driver's cab, and a whistle switch and a footrest are installed on the footrest under the console. There are electrical side cabinets and escape windows on both sides of the driver's cab. The cabinet on the left is equipped with a cab switch and auxiliary seat, and the cabinet on the right is equipped with a control panel and a fire extinguisher. The driver's cab switchboard is arranged on the left rear end wall of the driver's cab. Headlights and marker lights are installed in front of the driver's cab. Three LED downlights are installed on the top of the cab. The front glass of the front window of the driver's cab adopts a high-impact transparent electric-heat laminated safety glass. The side glass is tinted electric heating laminated safety glass. The front window of the driver's cab is equipped with an electric wiper and a manual sunshade device.

The driver's cab console is the main human machine interaction device in the driver's cab of the EMUs, and the driver realizes the main control of the train through it. The equipment layout of the cab console is shown in Fig.3.6, and the equipment names and functions are shown in Tab.3.1.

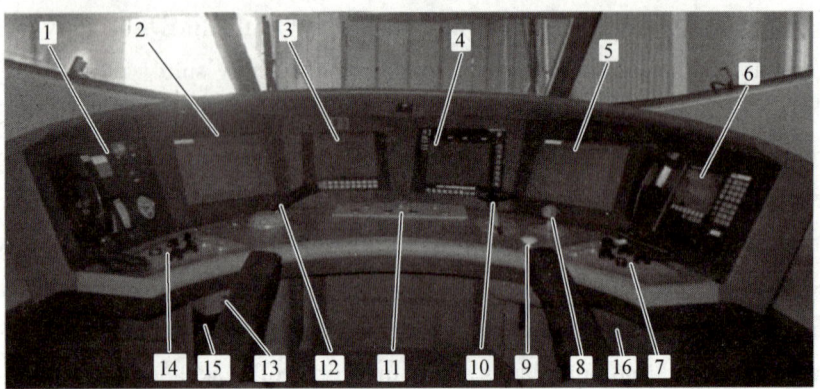

Fig.3.6 The Equipment Layout of The Cab Console

Tab.3.1 The Equipment Names and Functions of the Cab Console

No.	Name	Function
1	Instrument display panel	Pressure gauge, voltmeter, wiper switch, microphone printer, alert lights
2	EMUs information display monitor	EMUs information control status display
3	LKJ-2000 indicator	Provide optimization operation functions such as the display of Chinese characters and graphic curves
4	ATP speed indicator	Display EMUs speed
5	EMUs information display monitor	EMUs information control status display
6	CIR indicator, wireless microphone, door close signal lamp and door malfunction signal lamp	① Functions of GSM-R dispatching communication, general data transmission, application operation, status display and voice prompt; ② call outside; ③ Whether all doors are closed or not; ④ Display the status of operation, braking, door, etc
7	Right switch panel	Open and close the right door button, monitor speaker switch, sunshade switch, cab lights switch
8	Reversing handle	Set the running direction of the EMUs, which is divided into three gears: front, off and rear
9	Alarm manual switch	Manual switch for driver alertness system

Continue

No.	Name	Function
10	Traction handle	Set the traction force, which is divided into p1-p10.
11	Central switch panel	VCB on / off, reset, emergency reset, pantograph lowering and other function buttons
12	Brake handle	Set the braking force. which is divided into operation, B1-B7, fast, pull-out position
13	Emergency braking press	Emergency pull over
14	Left switch panel	Electric heating switch, air conditioning system switches, left door opening and closing buttons
15	Broadcast microphone	Broadcast to passengers in the EMUs
16	Equipment cabin access door	In order to enter the equipment cabin and front hatches

3.3 EMUs Body Maintenance

In the level I maintenance of the EMUs, the maintenance of the car body can be divided into two parts: inside and outside the car. The maintenance on the outside of the car body is usually carried out when the EMUs is powered off, while the maintenance on the inside of the car body usually needs to be carried out when the EMUs is powered on. The main maintenance tools used are: helmet, flashlight, walkie-talkie, steel ruler, cotton cloth, feeler gauge, ratchet wrench, and four corner keys. When the EMUs has no electricity, the maintenance items of the car body are as shown in Tab.3.2.

Tab.3.2 Maintenance Guide of Car body (Power off)

No.	Maintenance item	Maintenance guide	
1	Head car cover	① The wiper is in good appearance and without damage; ② The appearance of the headlight cover is in good condition without damage; ③ The windshield is not damaged; ④ The appearance of the opening and closing cover is in good condition, and there is no deformation or damage	Head car cover

Continue

No.	Maintenance item	Maintenance guide	
2	Front hatch	① All parts of the bottom front hatch are complete, without deformation or damage; ② The bolts are installed firmly and the anti-loosening marks are not misaligned	Front hatch
3	Underbody pipeline	① There are no cracks and leaks in the air pipes under the vehicle, and the installation is in good condition; ② The connecting pipes at the bottom of the vehicle are not damaged, the insulating rubber is not damaged, and the fixing is good	Underbody pipeline
4	Cab A/C condensing fan	① The fan cover and impeller are not damaged, broken or deformed. Check that there is no foreign matter inside the fan; ② The cover bolts are installed firmly, and the anti-loosening marks are not misaligned; ③ The bottom plate has no cracks and obvious deformation, and the aluminum honeycomb structure inside the plate is not exposed; ④ Use a ratchet wrench to check that the bottom plate lock is not loose	Cab A/C condensing fan
5	Common bottom plate	① The bottom plate has no cracks and obvious deformation, and the aluminum honeycomb structure inside the plate is not exposed; ② Use a ratchet wrench to check that the bottom plate lock is not loose	Common bottom plate

Continue

No.	Maintenance item	Maintenance guide	
6	Traction converter bottom plate	① The bottom plate has no cracks and obvious deformation; ② The bolts of each part are installed firmly, and the anti-loosening marks are not misaligned	Traction converter bottom plate
7	Doppler radar bottom plate	① The bottom plate has no obvious deformation and cracks, and the aluminum honeycomb structure inside the plate is not exposed; ② There is no crack at the stress concentration around the bottom plate opening; ③ Use a ratchet wrench to check that the bottom plate lock is not loose	Doppler radar bottom plate
8	Power terminal box lower cover	The cover plate is installed in good condition, the bolts are installed tightly and the anti-loosening marks are not dislocated	Power terminal box lower cover
9	Drain	① There is no mechanical damage to the drain outlet, it is well fixed, and there is no blockage; ② The fastening bolts are installed firmly, and the anti-loosening marks are not misaligned; ③ There is no defect or fall off of the cold protection layer	Drain

073

Continue

No.	Maintenance item	Maintenance guide	
10	Traction transformer bottom plate	① The bottom plate has no obvious deformation and cracks; ② The bolts are installed firmly, and the anti-loosening marks are not misaligned	Traction transformer bottom plate
11	Auxiliary converter bottom plate	① The bottom plate has no obvious deformation and cracks; ② The bolts are installed firmly, and the anti-loosening marks are not misaligned	Auxiliary converter bottom plate
12	Air compressor bottom plate	① The bottom plate has no obvious deformation and cracks, and the aluminum honeycomb structure inside the plate is not exposed; ② There is no crack at the stress concentration around the bottom plate opening; ③ Use a ratchet wrench to check that the bottom plate lock is not loose	Air compressor bottom plate

When the power-off maintenance of the EMUs is completed, the staff must confirm that there are no operators under the car body and on the roof. After confirming that the power supply safety conditions are met, go through the catenary power supply procedures, and raise the pantograph of the EMUs. When the EMUs is powered on, the maintenance of the car body in the level I maintenance is mainly to maintenance the parts inside or on both sides of the car body and the specific maintenance items are as shown in Tab.3.3.

Tab.3.3 Maintenance Guide of Car body (Power on)

No.	Maintenance item	Maintenance guide	
1	Car door	① All doors in the car are in good appearance and operate normally; ② All parts of the platform compensator are not damaged and operate normally	Car door
2	Passenger compartment facilities	① The appearance and installation status of the floor, top plate, mounting plate, seat, curtain, coffee table, luggage rack, and garbage bin are in good condition, and the window glass is not leaking or damaged; ② Seat number plate, coat hook, small table, appearance and installation are in good condition. Each handrail is firmly installed and in good condition; ③ There is no abnormal sound or smell in the car; ④ The appearance of the information display screen is normal and the display is normal. The emergency switch in good condition; ⑤ The air-conditioning in the passenger compartment is well ventilated and the temperature is normal	First class seat Second class seat
3	Lighting lamps	The appearance and installation state of each lamp are in good condition, the color of the lamp is the same, and the lamp is not extinguished	Lighting lamps

Continue

No.	Maintenance item	Maintenance guide	
4	Fire extinguisher	① The fire extinguisher is fully equipped and in good condition; ② The regular inspection of the fire extinguisher has not expired, and the pressure is normal	Fire Extinguisher
5	Sanitary equipment	① The toilet, sink, toilet paper holder, mirror, toilet device, flush button and other facilities have good appearance and no peculiar smell; ② The toilet door switch works well	Lavatory pan Toilet
6	Electric tea stove	The electric tea stoves of each car are firmly installed and function well, and each indicator light shows normal	Electric tea stove

Continue

No.	Maintenance item	Maintenance guide
7	Catering area and bar counter	Bar cushions and bar equipment are not loose or damaged Table Bar counter
8	Kitchen equipment	① The water supply module filter element is clean and free of dirt; ② The opening degree of the throttle valve of the water supply module is adjusted in place, and the pipeline pressure meets the regulations; ③ The ice shovel of the ice maker is clean and works well Kitchen equipment
9	Film and television system	The film and television system is well-equipped and in good working condition Display
10	Crew room	① The communication performance of the contact phone in the crew room is good; ② The appearance of the monitoring display is in good condition, the state is good, and the display is normal; ③ The seat is installed firmly without damage; ④ Other equipment in the crew room is in good condition and functions normally Crew room

Continue

No.	Maintenance item	Maintenance guide	
11	Power distribution cabinet	① The appearance of each power distribution cabinet is in good condition; ② The display of each power distribution cabinet is normal and the lock is good	Power distribution cabinet
12	Shutters	① The hinge, gate plate and spherical window hook base of the shutter are firm; ② There are no cracks or damage to the blades and frames of the shutters	Shutters
13	Cab equipment	① Monitor the appearance of the monitor and the display is good; ② The driver's seat is firmly installed and the lift is in good condition; ③ Indoor air conditioning, electric heating and lighting are good; ④ The indoor glass is not damaged. The wipers work well and the water spray is normal. The wiper rubber is undamaged	Driver console Driver seat — Switch

Continue

No.	Maintenance item	Maintenance guide	
14	Contact telephone	Confirm that the communication and broadcasting performance of each vehicle's contact telephone is good	Contact telephone
15	Head car skirt	① Check that the skirt lock is not loose with the four-corner key; ② The shut-off valve of the main air duct, the shut-off valve of the train pipe, and the cover plate of the sand injection port are well locked	Head car skirt
16	Traction motor cooling fan	Confirm that the traction motor cooling fan is working without abnormal noise	Traction motor cooling fan
17	Oil filler skirt	There is no loosening of the oil filling port skirt, the bolts are installed tightly, and the anti-loosening marks are not misaligned	Oil filler skirt / Skirt bolts

079

Continue

No.	Maintenance item	Maintenance guide	
18	A/C condenser skirt	The skirt plate is installed firmly, and the pedal is not loose	A/C condenser skirt
19	Exterior wall of car body	① Exterior wall panels, glass, and side doors are not deformed or damaged. ② The paint on the car body has no serious scratches and peeling off	Exterior wall
20	External display	The appearance of the external display screen is normal, and the information display is normal	External display
21	Common skirt	① The skirt board is installed in good condition and not loose; ② Check that there is no looseness of the skirt lock with the four-corner key	Common skirt

Continue

No.	Maintenance item	Maintenance guide
22	Bogie skirt	① Check that the skirt lock is not loose with the four-corner key; ② The apron is installed with angle iron, hooks without deformation, bolts installed tightly, and anti-loosening marks are not misaligned Bogie skirt Hanger
23	water inlet cover	① The cover of the water injection port is well locked, and the cover lock works well; ② There is no looseness at the shaft of the cover plate Water inlet cover
24	Gangways and jumper cables	① The appearance of the gangway at the connection of the car end has no cracks, no falling blocks, and no deformation; ② The jumper cables between the carriages are complete, without damage and without cuts. The anti-loosening marks of the cable connection terminal bolts are notmisaligned Gangways Jumper cables

Continue

No.	Maintenance item	Maintenance guide
25	Sewage outlet cover	① The cover plate of the sewage outlet is well locked, and the locking mechanism works well; ② There is no looseness at the shaft of the cover plate, and the gas spring works well Sewage outlet cover
26	EMUs control system test	① Brake test: The brake control function of the EMUs is good; ② Side door test: Operate the open and close buttons on the cab console respectively to ensure that the side door switch is in good condition; ③ Air conditioning test: There is no fault information on the display screen of the results of the start of the air conditioning of each vehicle; ④ Wiper test: the wiper nozzle operates normally, and the water level of the glass meets the requirements; ⑤ The whistle high-bass function test: the whistle is in good working condition, the ball valve is locked, and the exhaust function is normal Drives console

Homework

1. What are the common materials of EMUs body?

2. What are the advantages of using aluminum alloy as the body material of the EMUs?

3. What are the methods of lightening the body of the EMUs?

4. What are the components of the EMUs body?

5. What equipment does the CRH2 EMUs driver's cab console have?

6. Briefly describe the maintenance content of the EMUs body.

Chapter 4

EMUs Bogie Structure and Maintenance

> Learning objectives

- Know the EMUs bogie design principles.
- Know the classification of bogies of the EMUs bogie.
- Understand the EMUs bogie structure.
- Familiar with EMUs bogie composition and maintenance.

4.1 Bogie Design Principles

Bogie is one of the most important components of EMUs. Whether its structure is reasonable directly affects the running quality, dynamic performance and driving safety of EMUs. Due to the different history and background of railway development in different countries, as well as the differences in technical conditions, the structural types of high-speed bogies developed by different countries are also quite different. However, the consensus on design principles and practical experience have resulted in many similarities in the form of high-speed bogies, such as the use of air spring suspension system, elastic positioning of wear-free axle box, disc brake based composite braking system. According to the design experience of high-speed bogies, there are the following design principles:

(1) High flexible spring suspension system is used to obtain good vibration performance. This kind of high flexibility air spring can show excellent performance under the speed of 380 km/h.

(2) High strength and lightweight bogie structure is adopted to reduce the dynamic interaction between wheel and rail.

(3) Composite braking system is adopted for foundation braking device.

(4) All kinds of measures can effectively restrain the hunting motion of bogie and improve the critical speed of bogie hunting motion.

(5) The driving device adopts simple, practical, reliable and mature structure to minimize the unsprung weight, so as to improve the action force between wheel and rail and improve the stability of high-speed operation.

The following will take the bogie of the CRH3 EMUs as an example to introduce. The technical parameters of the CRH3 EMUs are shown in Tab.4.1.

Tab.4.1　Main Technical Parameters of CRH3 EMUs Bogie

Technical parameters	Bogie	
	Motor car	trailer
Maximum operating speed/(km/h)	350	
Maximum test speed/(km/h)	380	
Gauge /mm	1435	
Fixed wheelbase /mm	2500	
Distance between backs of the wheel flanges /mm	1353(0,+2)	
Center distance of air spring/mm	1900	
Wheel diameter (new/old)/mm	920/830	920/860
Maximum static axle weight/t	$17(1\pm4\%)$	$17(1\pm4\%)$
mechanical brake	Wheel-disc brake	Axle-disc brake
Bogie quality/kg	$\leqslant 10\ 000$	$\leqslant 7\ 500$

4.2　The Composition of Bogie

Generally, the bogies of EMUs can be divided into motor bogies and trailer bogies. The structures of motor bogie and trailer bogie are basically the same. EMUs bogies include: bogie frame, axle box guidance, wheelset, primary suspension, secondary suspension, driving device, foundation brake device. The biggest difference between a motor bogie and a trailer bogie is that the trailer bogie has no driving device. The motor bogie is shown in Fig.4.1, and the trailer bogie is shown in Fig.4.2.

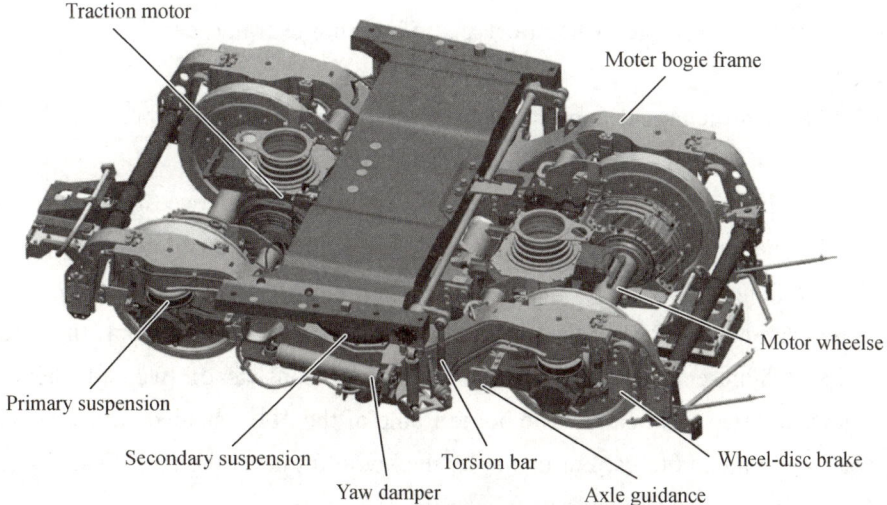

Fig.4.1 Overview of motor bogie

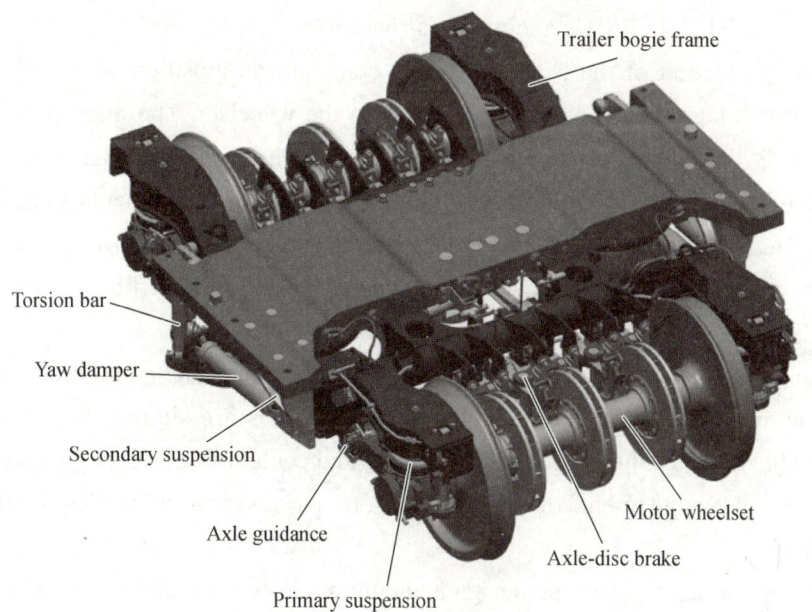

Fig.4.2 Overview of trailer bogie

4.2.1 Bogie Frame

The bogie frame is the skeleton of the bogie and the bogie frame combines the various parts of the bogie into a whole to connect the components of the bogie and transmit forces in all directions. The bogie frame is generally composed of left and right side beams and one or several across beams (or end beams) and installation or suspension supports for various related equipment. According to the number of across beams or end beams that make up the frame, the basic structural types of the bogie frame can be divided into the following 5 types.

(1) H-shaped structure: It consists of two side beams and a cross beam in the middle. The bogie frame of the CRH2 EMUs adopts this structure.

(2) "口" (Chinese character)-shaped structure: It consists of two side beams and two end beams. The bogie frame of ICE1 high-speed train from German adopts this structure.

(3) "日" (Chinese character)-shaped structure: It consists of two side beams, a middle beam and two end beams. Part of the bogie frame of the CRH1 EMUs adopts this structure.

(4) "目" (Chinese character)-shaped structure: It consists of two side beams, two middle beams and two end beams. The bogie frame of the "目"-shaped structure is mainly used in traditional locomotives. For example, the bogie frame of the DF_4 diesel locomotive and the SS_3 electric locomotive adopts this structure.

(5) II-shaped structure: It consists of two side beams and two middle beams. The bogie frame of the CRH5 EMUs adopts this structure.

The main function of the side beam is to constrain the position of the wheelset and transmit vertical, lateral and longitudinal forces to the wheelset. The main function of the across beam is to ensure the rigidity of the frame in the horizontal plane, maintain the parallelism of each axis and provide installation positions for components such as traction motors. The number of across beams and side beams is mainly set according to the strength and rigidity of the frame and the installation and suspension of specific components of the bogie.

The bogie frames of the CRH3 EMUs are of modular design. The bogie frames for motor bogie are shown in Figure 4.3. The major modules are similar in all bogies. The individual adjustment of the bogies to the weights and centers of gravity of each car as well as the individual adjustment of the suspension springs results in optimum running characteristics.

The bogie frame is a H-shape design and consists of two welded box-section side sills that are interconnected via two tubular transoms. The frame is manufactured mainly of low alloy high strength weathering steel sheets. some bogie frames are equipped with antenna supports. These antenna supports are fixed to the bogie frame by bolts. All necessary brackets for mounting parts are welded on the bogie frame without causing additional or excessive stresses. Welded on the side beam are the axle box guidance seat, the primary vertical damper holder, the primary spring positioning seat, the secondary air spring positioning seat, the antiroll torsion bar seat, the yaw damper holder, the bogie hanger and brake beam. Welded on the across beam are traction link seat, gearbox hanger, traction motor hanger. Due to the different equipment, the trailer bogie frames are provided without the brackets for traction motors and gear unit reaction bars. The trailer bogies are equipped with brackets for the wheel brake discs. The bogie frames for trailer bogie are shown in Fig.4.4. The bogie frames for motor bogie and trailer bogie are not interchangeable.

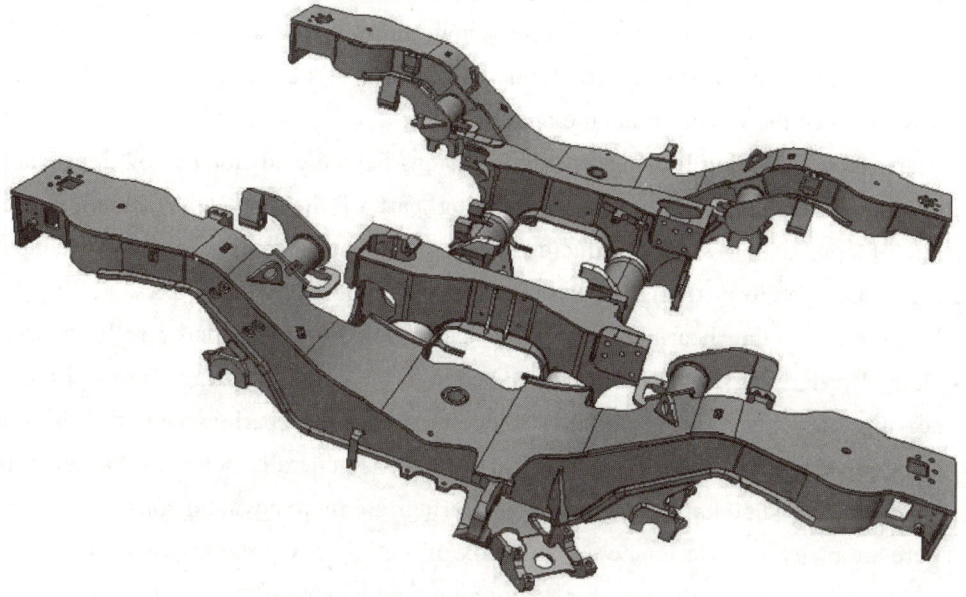

Fig.4.3　Motor Bogie Frames

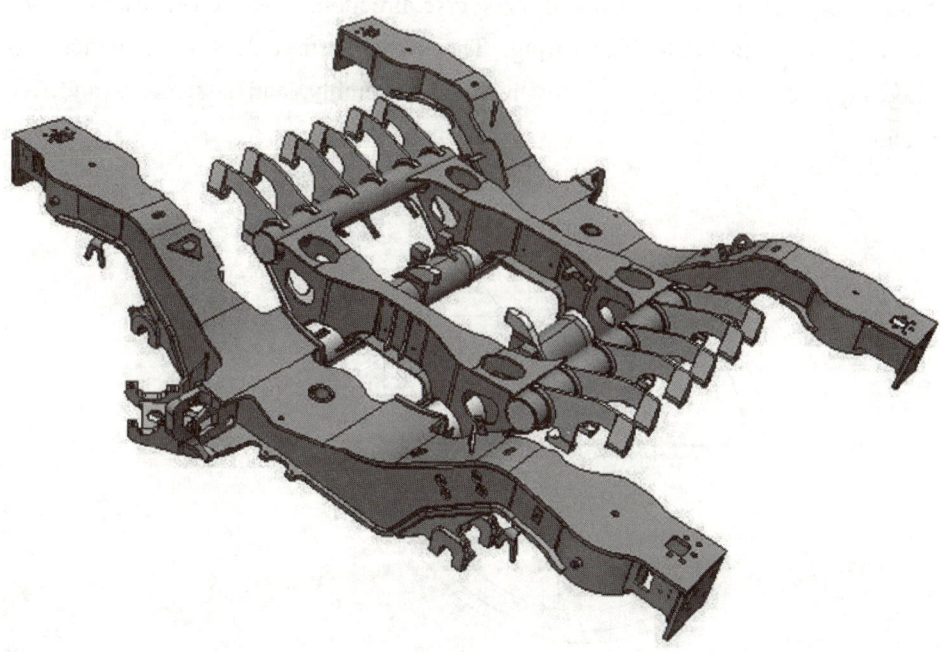

Fig.4.4　Trailer Bogie Frames

4.2.2 Axle Box Guidance

Axle box guidance is the key component to realize both connection and mutual movement of wheelset and bogie frame. The axle box guidance is the movable joint connecting the wheelset and the bogie frame, which transmits the traction force (or braking force), lateral force and vertical force, and realizes the vertical movement and traverse movement between the wheelset and the bogie frame.

Compared with sliding bearings, rolling bearings have the advantages of significantly reducing the working conditions of the running part of the vehicle, reducing inertial accidents of combustion shafts, reducing maintenance and repair work, and reducing operating costs. Therefore, all high-speed trains use rolling bearing axle boxes.

The types of rolling bearings are: cylindrical roller bearings, tapered roller bearings and spherical roller bearings. The axle box bearings of high-speed trains use cylindrical roller bearings and tapered roller bearings. Since tapered roller bearings have the ability to transmit large axial loads while bearing radial loads, it is generally believed that when the EMUs speed exceeds 250 km/h, tapered roller bearings are more advantageous.

There are many ways to locate the axle box of the bogie. On the high-speed train, the swivel arm axle box is usually used for positioning, and its structural schematic diagram is shown in Fig.4.5. The swivel arm axle box guidance is to connect the axle box and the frame side beam in the longitudinal and transverse directions, and the vertical positioning is mainly realized by the axle box spring. The swivel arm axle box guidance has the advantages of simple structure, convenient disassembly and assembly, and reliable performance.

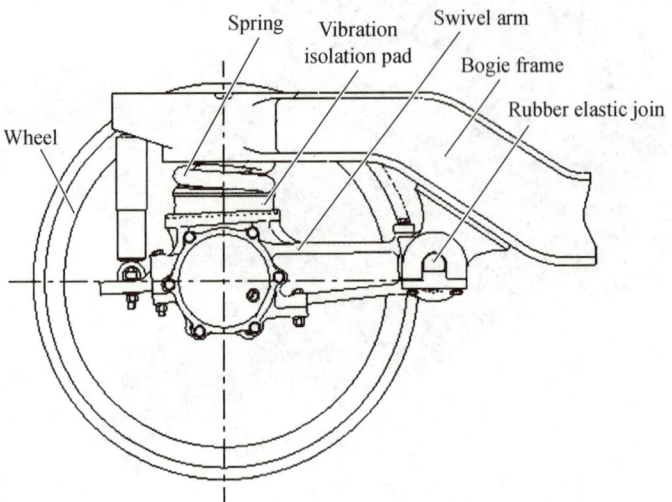

Fig.4.5　Structural Schematic Diagram of Swivel Arm Axle Box

The axle boxes of CRH3 EMUs are made from cast iron and designed for use with roller taper bearings. The positioning method of the axle box adopts the swivel arm type. The swivel arm and the swivel arm hoop are marked with steel stamps, which must be used in pairs and are not interchangeable. Change of the wheel set is possible without dismounting the bearings. The axle bearing boxes have a divided design. The lower halve of the bearing box can be dismounted for the wheel set exchange. Axle box of CRH3 EMUs is shown in Fig.4.6.

Fig.4.6　Axle Box of CRH3 EMUs

The shaft end is equipped with antiskid transmitters, speed transmitters, CTCS sensor, earthing contacts. According to the different installation devices, the front cover of the axle box is divided into 5 types: D, A, C, F and H, as shown in Fig.4.7 – 4.11. The bearing life calculation adopts L10, and the service life is greater than or equal to 3.5 million km.

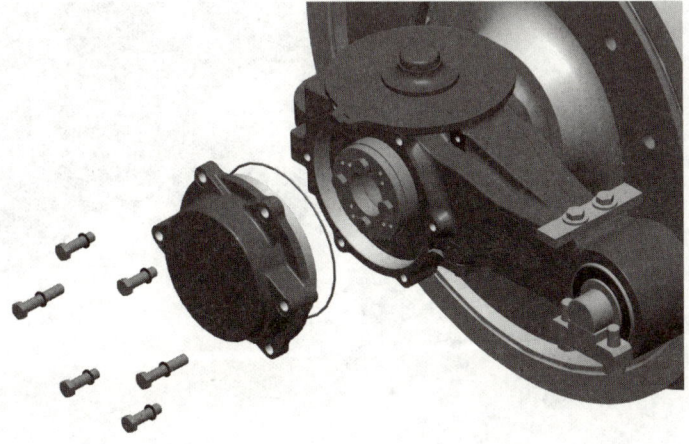

Fig.4.7　D-type Axle Box Cover

Fig.4.8　A-type Axle Box Cover

Fig.4.9　C-type Axle Box Cover

Fig.4.10　F-type Axle Box Cover

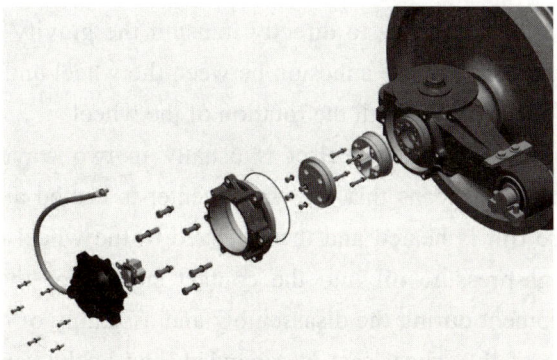

Fig.4.11　H-type Axle Box Cover

4.2.3　Wheelset

A high-speed train wheelset is generally composed of axle shafts and wheels. The axle shafts are hollow axle shafts, and the wheels are integral wheels. In addition, high-speed train wheelsets can be divided into motor wheelsets and trailer wheelsets. the motor axle shafts are equipped with gearboxes and wheel-disc brakes, while the trailer axle shafts are often equipped with axle-disc brakes. The motor axle shaft is shown in Fig.4.12 and the trailer axle shaft is shown in Fig.4.13.

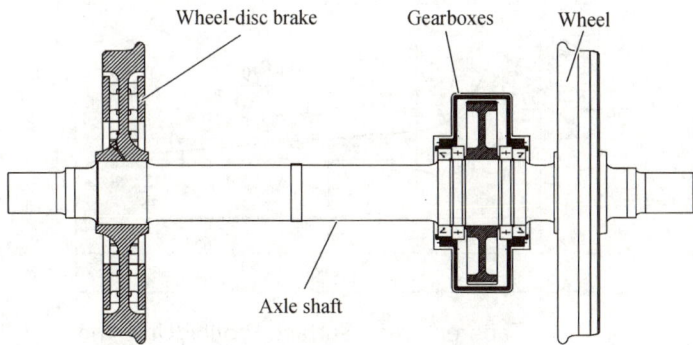

Fig.4.12　Motor Axle Shaft

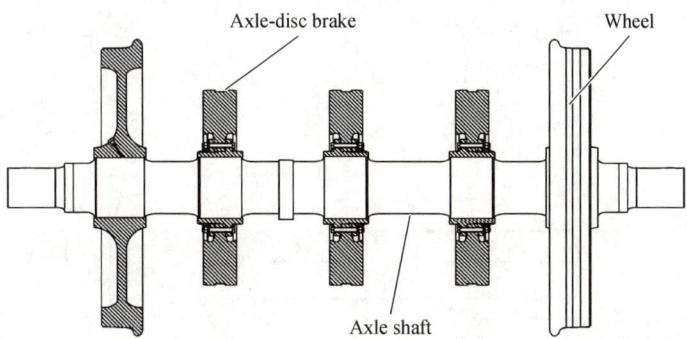

Fig.4.13　Trailer Axle Shaft

The function of the wheelset is to directly transmit the gravity to the track, generate traction or braking force through the adhesion between the wheel and the track, and realize the train operating on the track through the rotation of the wheel.

The assembly process of the wheelset is usually in two ways: heat shrink fit and hydraulic fit. heat shrink fit means that the wheel center is heated and then sleeved to the axle shaft, and the tire rim is heated and then sleeved to the wheel center. Hydraulic suit refers to injecting high-pressure oil into the contact surface of the wheel seat through special hydraulic equipment during the disassembly and assembly of the wheel and the axle shaft, so that the hole of the wheel seat is expanded, and at the same time, the wheel is pressed in or out by applying axial thrust.

The study of the wheel-rail relationship is an important part of the wheel parameter design of the EMUs. The contact part of the wheel with the top surface of the rail is called the wheel tread. The protruding part of the wheel tread in contact with the inner side of the rail is called the flange, and its function is to prevent the wheel from derailing. In order to make the wheelset run smoothly on the rail, smoothly pass the curve, reduce the wheel wear, and prolong the number of kilometers on the wheel, the tread surface should have a reasonable shape. There are two types of treads: tapered tread surface and wear tread surface, as shown in Fig.4.14 and 4.15.

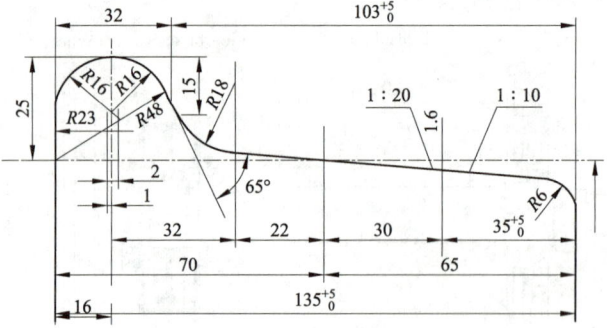

Fig.4.14　Tapered Tread Surface Profile (Unit: mm)

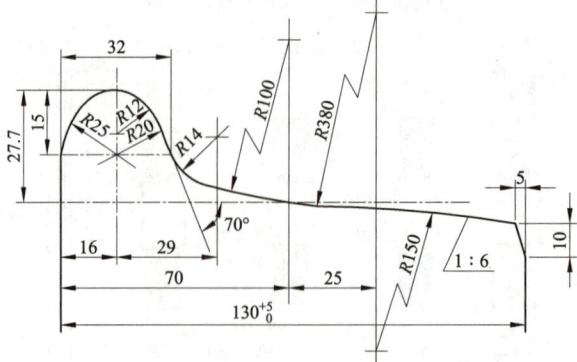

Fig.4.15　Wear Tread Surface Profile (Unit: mm)

The tapered treads are sloped to reduce longitudinal wheel slip as the train passes curves. When the train operates in a straight line, the wheelset can be kept automatically centered to avoid the eccentric wear caused by the contact of the wheel flange with the rail. However, as the operating speed of the train increases, the inclination of the tapered tread causes the bogie to intensify the yaw motion, which affects the lateral stability and stability of the train, so the tread slope should not be too large.

A section of tread with an inclination of 1:20 is often in contact with the rail, and wears quickly, which is easy to form a depression on the tread, and the wheelset may jump violently when entering a turnout or a small radius curve. To avoid this, there is a 1:10 slope on the outside of the 1:20 slope, which only touches the rail surface on small radius curves.

For high-speed trains in Japan and France, in order to improve the anti-yaw motion of the train, the tapered tread with a slope of 1:20 is changed to a slope of 1:40. However, after the tread wears out during use, the slope increases significantly, requiring frequent maintenance to keep the original shape of the tread as much as possible.

The contact range between the tapered tread and the rail is very narrow, and local wear occurs on this narrow contact area, making the tread concave. However, after the tread reaches a certain degree of concave shape, the shape is relatively stable and the wear becomes slower. If the tread shape is directly designed as a wear shape (concave), the wheel-rail contact is relatively stable at the beginning and wears slowly. This kind of tread is called a wear tread.

Compared with the tapered tread, the main features of the wear tread are as follows:

(1) On a straight line, the contact part between the tread and the arc-shaped rail head is not a cone but an arc-shaped concave surface.

(2) There is a small arc at the connection between the flange root and the tread, and a transition arc is added at the connection between the small arc and the tread for wear tread. The transition arc avoids the two-point contact between the rail and the tread and wheel flange.

The advantages of wear treads are:

(1) The maintenance mileage is extended and the wheel cutting amount during maintenance is reduced.

(2) Under the same contact stress, a larger axle load is allowed.

(3) Reduced wheel flange wear on the curve.

The disadvantage of the wear tread is that the equivalent slope is large, which is not good for the yaw stability of the train. Therefore, for high-speed train, yaw damper must be used to ensure sufficient stability of the train.

The bogie wheelset of CRH3 EMUs uses integral wheels. The new wheel rolling circle diameter is 920 mm. When worn to the limit, the diameter of the motor bogie wheel is 830 mm, and the diameter of the trailer bogie wheel is 860 mm.

The axle shafts of the CRH3 EMUs are hollow axle shafts with a hollow diameter of 30 mm. The axle shafts are designed for a fatigue life of 20 years. The axle shaft material is A4T and the wheel material is R8T.

The wheels are crimped to the axle shafts by means of interference press fitting, and the wheels are unloaded by means of oil injection.

The axle shaft of the CRH3 motor bogie has a bracket for installing gears, but no bracket for installing an axle-disc brake. A gear box and two wheel-disc brakes are installed on the axle shaft. The wheelsets of the CRH3 motor bogie is shown in Fig.4.16.

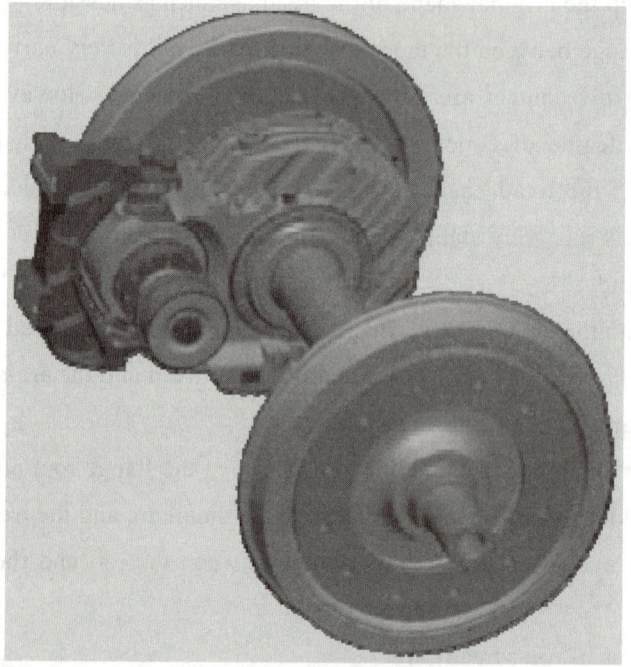

Fig.4.16　CRH3 Motor Wheelsets

Trailer bogie axle shafts have bracket for axle-disc brakes, but no bracket for installing a gear box. Three axle-disc brakes are installed on the axles shaft. The wheelsets of the CRH3 trailer bogie is shown in Fig.4.17.

Fig.4.17 CRH3 Trailer Wheelsets

The tread profile of the CRH3 EMUs is shown in Fig.4.18. The shape of the wheel tread can match the current track conditions, and the traction performance of the train can be optimized under the premise of ensuring the safety of train operation and the comfort of passengers on the train.

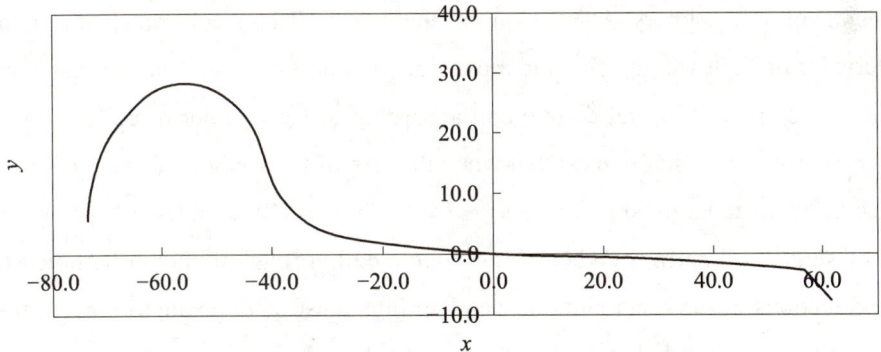

Fig.4.18 CRH3 Tread Profile in Plane Cartesian Coordinate System

4.2.4 Primary Suspension

The structure and parameters of the suspension device directly affect the operating quality of the high-speed train. A good suspension device can make the train operate smoothly, reduce vibration, and make passengers feel comfortable. At the same time, it can protect the equipment in the train and reduce the impact on the rail. Suspension devices can be divided into primary suspension and secondary suspension. The primary suspension is located between the bogie frame and the axle box, and the primary suspension includes a spring and a vertical damper, as shown in Fig.4.19.

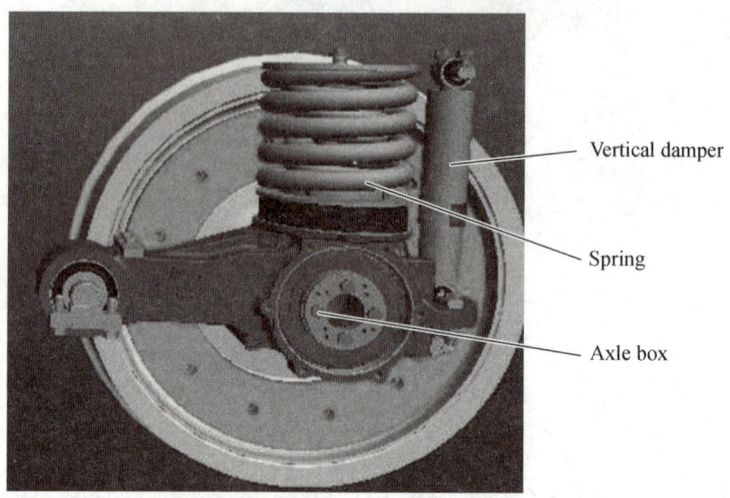

Fig.4.19　The Primary Suspension Components

　　The round spring is one of the most common and common springs, which is made of the elasticity of the steel itself. High-speed trains usually use steel circular springs as components of the primary suspension of the bogie. The steel round spring has the characteristics of light weight, flexible movement and no damping. The circular spring can be divided into single coil and double coil according to the number of coils of the spring. Single-coil springs are usually used, but when the size of the single-coil spring is limited by the space of the installation site or its spring bars are too thick, double-coil springs are used instead of single-coil springs. When using double coil springs, it should be noted that the rotation directions of the inner and outer coil springs must be opposite to prevent the small spring from being embedded in the large spring due to the vibration of the train.

　　The vertical damper of high-speed train is usually hydraulic damper. The hydraulic damper is composed of a piston, a cylinder, a piston valve, an oil inlet valve and various sealing rings. The working principle of the hydraulic shock absorber is to use the viscous resistance of the liquid to do negative work to absorb the vibration energy. The structure of the hydraulic damper is shown in Fig.4.20.

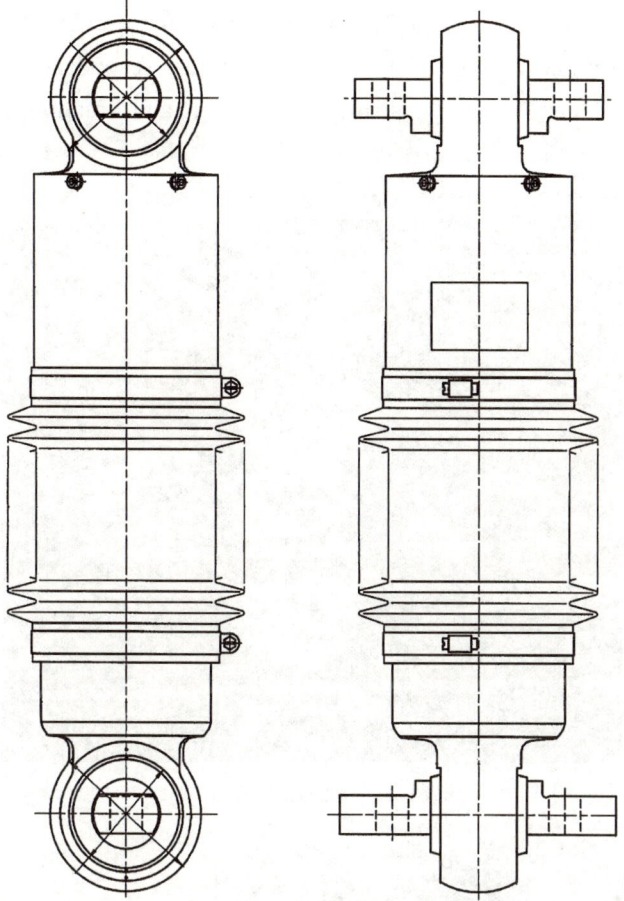

Fig.4.20 The Structure of the Hydraulic Damper

The CRH3 EMUs adopts double coil rigid spring, and the spring installation direction is marked in yellow. There is an emergency suspension device in the coil spring. Under the steel spring is a thick rubber pad with high flexibility to ensure sound and electrical insulation. The length of the positioning arm is 480mm. The positioning joint adopts an integrally vulcanized rubber joint. The nodal mandrel is positioned by an arc, as shown in Fig.4.21. Compared with the trapezoidal groove structure, it is easier to disassemble and install and the force is more uniform. And it is equipped with a wheelset emergency system to meet the design principle of fail-safe and reliable.

4.2.5 Secondary Suspension

The secondary suspension is used to transfer the vertical and horizontal forces between the car body and the bogie, so that the bogie can rotate relative to the car body when the train passes the curve, and further slow down the impact vibration between the car body and the bogie, and ensure the stability of the bogie. It includes secondary spring, damper in all directions, height control valve, antiroll torsion bar and traction device. Secondary suspension is shown in Fig.4.22.

Fig.4.21　Positioning Joint

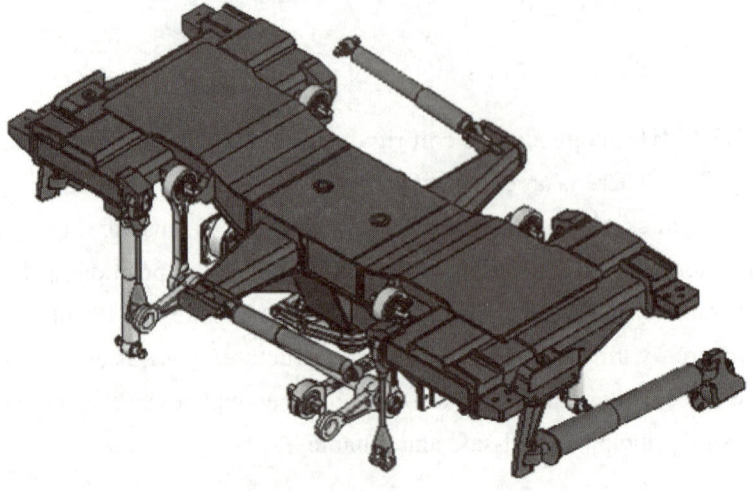

Fig.4.22　The Primary Suspension

1. Air Spring System

The air spring is an elastic body of a certain stiffness formed by sealing compressed air in a rubber membrane. The air spring system is arranged as a secondary stage between the bogie frame and the car body. Air spring system is shown in Fig4.23. The air spring system can be adjusted softly when the train is passing in a straight line and cushion the impact caused by the centrifugal force when the train is passing in a curve.

Fig.4.23 Air Spring System

Air spring system have the following properties:

(1) The air spring system has small stiffness and large equivalent static deflection, which can reduce the natural vibration frequency of the train.

(2) Compared to steel springs, Air springs have nonlinear characteristics. The air spring can be designed with matching elastic parameters according to the vibration performance of the train. During normal operation of the train, the vibration amplitude is small and the air spring stiffness is low. When the displacement of the train due to vibration is too large, the stiffness of the air spring increases significantly, which can limit the amplitude of the car body.

(3) The stiffness of the air springs can vary with the load. Therefore, when the train operates under different conditions of empty and loaded, the natural vibration frequency of the car body and the stability are almost same.

(4) When the air spring system and the height control valve are used together, the car body can keep the height of the train floor from the rail surface basically unchanged under different static loads.

(5) The air spring system can bear loads in three-dimensional directions at the same time. By using the lateral elastic characteristics of the air springs, the structural design of the bogie can be optimized and the weight of the bogie can be reduced.

(6) The air spring system has good performance of absorbing high frequency vibration and sound insulation.

However, the air spring system has the disadvantages of complex structure, many accessories, high manufacturing cost and complicated maintenance and repair. Therefore, it is generally only used for high-speed trains.

2. anti-roll torsion bar

The anti-roll torsion bar is mainly composed of a torsion bar, a support seat, a torsion beam and a connecting rod, as shown in Fig.4.24. The function of the anti-roll torsion bar is to restrain the car body from rolling relative to the bogie and improve the stability and comfort of the train. The anti-roll torsion bar is installed between the car body and the bogie frame, and the torsion bar is used to resist torsional deformation to restrain the rolling tendency of the car body.

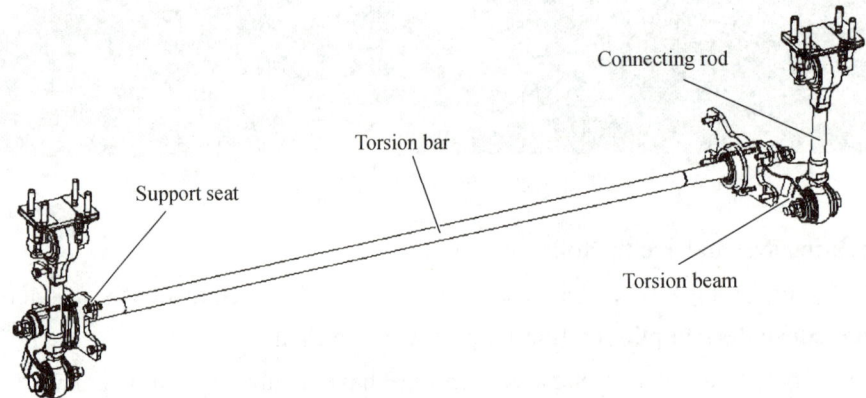

Fig.4.24   The anti-roll torsion bar structure

The working principle of the anti-roll torsion bar is that when the car body rolls, the two horizontally placed torsion beams act on the torsion bar with a mutually opposite force and moment respectively, so that the elastic torsion bar bears the torque and produces torsional elastic deformation, which acts as a torsion spring. The reaction torque of the torsion spring is always opposite to the direction of the angular displacement of the rolling body to restrain the rolling motion of the car body. However, when the vehicle body is normally vertically vibrated (the left and right vehicle bodies are displaced in the same direction but there is no roll). Since the bearing is installed in the torsion bar support, the left and right torsion beams only make the torsion bar rotate in the same direction, and do not function as a torsion spring, so it does not have an anti-rolling effect on the car body.

3. Height control valve

The height control valve is an important component in the air spring suspension device. Generally installed between the car body and the bogie. The height control valve can automatically adjust the pressure in the air spring according to the change of train load, and automatically maintain the function of maintaining a certain height between the car body and the bogie frame under different loads.

In addition, because the height control valve is used to keep the height of the vehicle body from the rail surface stable, the spring can be made very soft, and combined with the vibration characteristics of the air spring, a very comfortable ride quality can be obtained

4. Yaw damper

The yaw damper is one of the most important parts to ensure the stability of the train at high speed. As the EMUs travels along the track, the wheelset produces a characteristic movement with a tendency to increase in amplitude. The wheelset moves laterally on the one hand and rotates around the vertical axis passing through its center of mass on the other hand. The coupling of these two motions is called yaw motion.

In order to suppress the yaw motion of the EMUs, the yaw damper is installed longitudinally between the car body and the bogie frame, as shown in Fig.4.26. The yaw damper can greatly increase the critical speed of the train and greatly improve the operating stability of the EMUs.

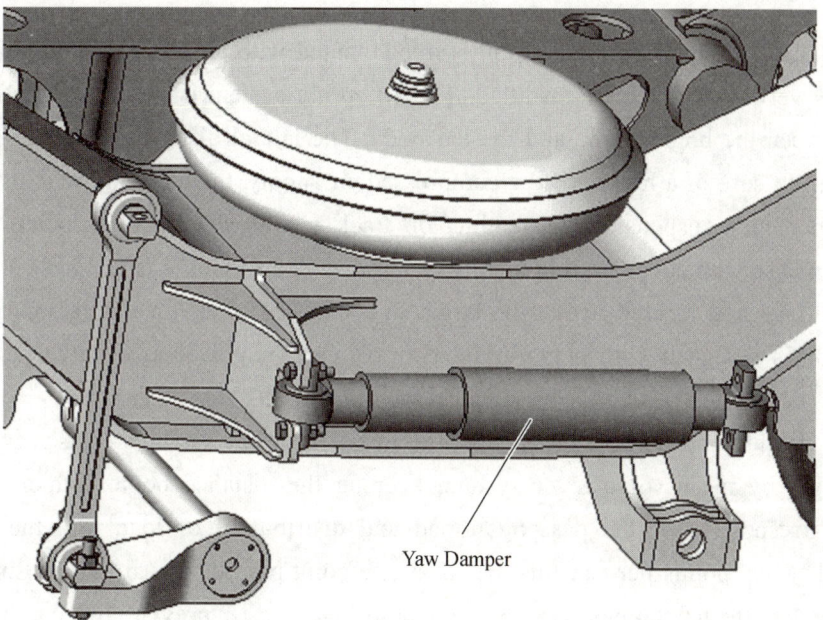

Fig.4.26　Yaw Damper

The secondary suspension of CRH3 EMUs:

The bogie connection to the car body bolster is provided by a pivot pin, fixed to the bolster by bolts. There are yaw damper mounts and torsion bar mounts on the car body bolster, as shown in Fig.4.27.

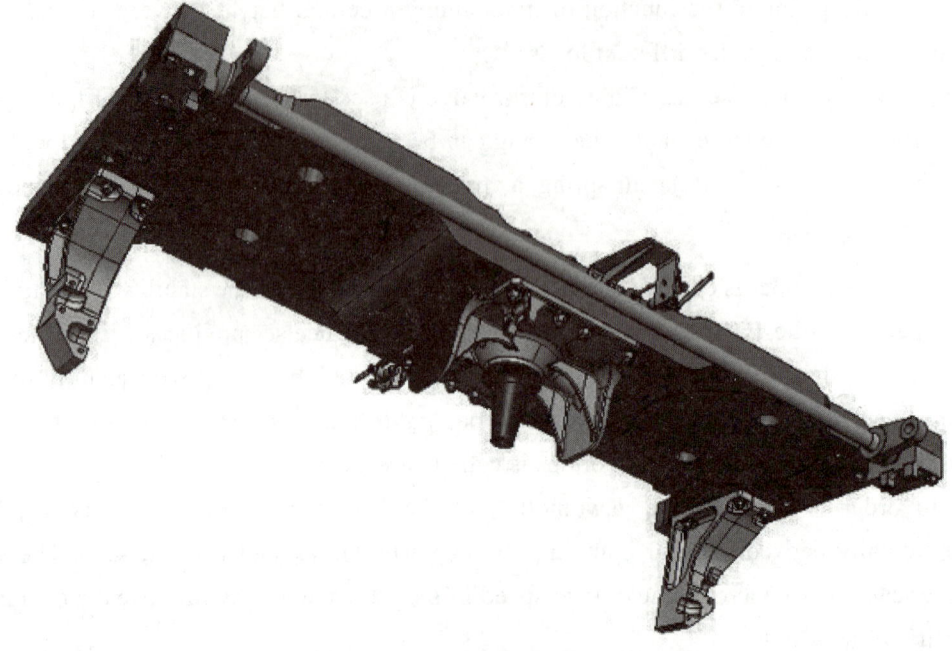

Fig.4.27　The Car Body Bolster System

The secondary vertical suspension is implemented with air springs, and no additional secondary vertical damper are installed. The air spring system is arranged as a secondary stage between the bogie frame and the car body. The lateral distance of the air springs is 1 900 mm. In case of a failure of the compressed air supply, the car body will settle to rest on its emergency suspension. Depending on track quality the travel velocity has to be reduced to ensure an adequate ride quality. A large extra air volume is directly connected to the air springs and located above the bogie in a cross member on the car body. The air suspension is designed with a two-point control. One height control valve per bogie is mounted.

One height control valve on each bogie, installed on the car bolster, is regulating the floor height by means of a lever system, keeping the distance bogie frame - car body constant irrespective of the passenger load and distribution of load. So, the height is measured at two points per car, this means at one point per bogie. All two air springs of a bogie are fed by the bogies own height control valve. To prevent the car body from excessive rolling due to curving and due to wind forces, an anti-roll bar has been provided.

This anti-roll torsion bar also assures transverse leveling of the car body. Vehicle height variations due to wheel wear (changes in diameter after wheel re-profiling) are adjusted by adjusting the length of the control rods between height control valves and bogie frame. This adjustment has to be done after every wheel re-profiling.

One anti-roll torsion bar is provided per bogie to limit the roll movements of the car body during curving and especially during high wind speeds. This anti-roll torsion bar consists of a torsion bar arrangement and two guide bars, connecting the torsion bar levers with the bogie frame.

CRH3 EMUs bogies are installed with 4 yaw dampers, 2 on each side, as shown in Fig.4.28. Considering the safety under fault conditions, the EMUs still has proper stability when a single yaw damper fails.

Fig.4.28 Yaw Damper of CRH3 EMUs

4.2.6 Driving Device

The driving device refers to the execution device that finally effectively transmits the energy generated by the power device on the motor bogie to the wheelset. For EMUs, the driving devices mainly include traction motors, axle gearboxes, couplings and transmission mechanisms, as shown in Fig.4.29.

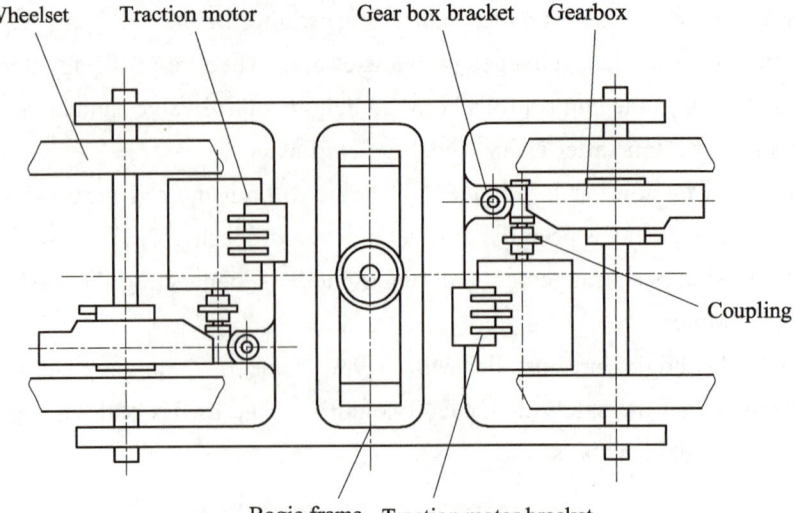

Fig.4.29　Schematic Diagram of the Structure of the Driving Device

The driving device is the most obvious feature that distinguishes the motor bogie from the trailer bogie, and it is also one of the most critical technologies for the motor bogie. Different forms of drive units are suitable for EMUs with different operating speed levels. According to the different suspension modes of the traction motor on the EMUs, the structure of the EMUs drive device can usually be divided into two types: frame-mounted motor driving system and carbody-mounted motor driving system type.

1. Frame-mounted motor driving system

Frame-mounted motor driving system means that the traction motor is completely mounted on the bogie frame, and its entire mass is borne by the bogie frame, without direct connection with the axle, and the driving torque is transmitted to the wheelset through a set of flexible transmission mechanisms. There are many transmission modes that cooperate with the frame-mounted motor. Among them, using WN coupling transmission type frame-mounted motor driving system has been widely used in the power decentralization type EMUs.

The WN coupling is composed of pinion, sleeve, spacer plate and rubber ring, as shown in Fig.4.30. The WN coupling belongs to the drum gear structure, and the structure is basically symmetrical from left to right. The two half-couplings are respectively press-fitted on the shaft head of the motor armature shaft and the pinion input shaft through keys or conical surfaces. Viewed from tip surface of the gear, each tooth flank is a drum shape. The tooth tip and tooth flank of the half coupling are arc-shaped, so the entire coupling is a double-live joint and is "flexible".

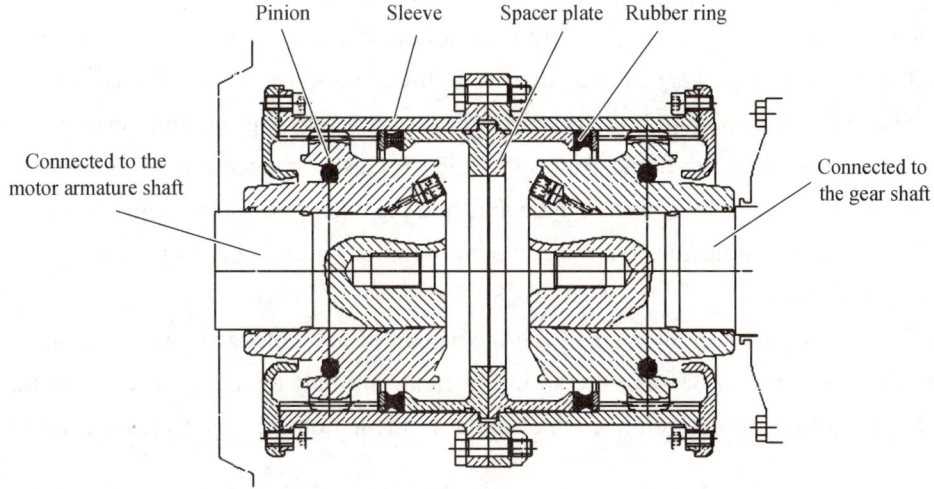

Fig.4.30 The structure of WN coupling.

The principle of the WN coupling transmission type frame-mounted motor driving system is to completely fix the traction motor to the across beam of the bogie frame by bolting. The output torque of the traction motor is transmitted to the driving pinion through the WN coupling, and the torque is transmitted to the driven large gear through the meshing of the gears, thereby driving the wheelsets to rotate. The driving device shown in Fig.4.31 is a WN coupling transmission type frame-mounted motor driving system.

Fig.4.31 The WN Coupling Frame-Mounted Motor Driving System

What needs special attention here is the mounted method of the gearbox. Unlike the mounted method of the motor, the gearbox is not completely mounted on the bogie frame. Instead, the driven large gear of the gearbox is directly press-fitted on the axle, while one end of the gearbox is mounted on the axle through a bearing, and the other end is mounted on the across beam of the bogie frame through an elastic hanger rod. About half of the entire mass of the gearbox is borne by the axle and the other half by the bogie frame.

WN coupling transmission type frame-mounted motor driving system has the following advantages:

(1) The unsprung weight is small (all the weight of the motor is mounted on the across beam of bogie frame to become the sprung weight, but half of the weight of the traction gear box is still unsprung weight), which reduces the action force between the wheel and rail.

(2) The working conditions of the traction motor are greatly improved.

(3) Compared with other frame-mounted motor driving system and carbody-mounted motor driving system, the structure of WN coupling transmission type frame-mounted motor driving system is much simpler.

(4) Simple disassembly and assembly, convenient maintenance and repair.

It is precisely because of the relatively simple structure of the WN coupling type frame-mounted motor driving system, coupled with the fact that the power decentralization EMUs adopts a light-weight AC asynchronous traction motor. Therefore, this kind of driving device has been widely used in high-speed EMUs. In China's high-speed railway system, the CRH1, CRH2 and CRH3 EMUs all use the WN coupling type frame-mounted motor driving system.

2. Carbody–mounted motor driving system

Carbody-mounted motor driving system means that the traction motor is completely installed under the chassis of the car body. The entire mass of the traction motor is borne by the chassis of the car body, and the driving torque is transmitted by the transmission mechanism. In the carbody-mounted motor driving system, there are many ways to design the transmission mechanism. However, the cardan shaft can better compensate the relative movement in all directions between the traction motor and the axle gearbox while transmitting the driving torque. Therefore, the cardan shaft is usually used as the transmission mechanism to transmit the driving torque.

Cardan shaft transmission type carbody-mounted motor driving system usually consists of an axle gearbox, a cardan shaft, a safety device and a traction motor. The traction motor is completely suspended on the underframe of the car body through the mounting bracket, as shown in Figure 4.32. The traction motor transmits the torque to the axle gearbox through the flexible cardan shaft. The transmission structure is shown in Fig.4.33.

Fig.4.32　Mounted Position of Traction Motor

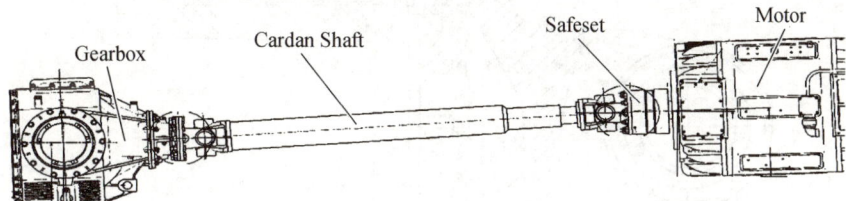

Fig.4.33　Cardan Shaft Type Carbody-Mounted Motor Driving System

The axle gearbox is mounted on the axle through two pairs of bearings, and a balance boom located at the bottom of the box is connected to the bogie frame beam. The main function of the balance boom is to provide support for the gear box and balance the external torque transmitted by the cardan shaft. The gearbox structure is shown in Fig.4.34.

Fig.4.34　Mounted Position of the Gearbox

107

The safeset is press-fitted on the traction motor shaft, and the safeset is connected to the cardan shaft in the transmission line by means of studs, and rotates together with the motor shaft to drive the cardan shaft. The function of the safeset is to protect the cardan shaft when the gearbox or motor fails to generate excessive torque. The structure of the safety set is shown in Fig.4.35.

The safeset has a hydraulic torque setting system, and by adjusting the hydraulic pressure, the release torque can be set to the desired level. When the preset torque is exceeded, the coupling on the safeset slips off, releasing the oil pressure in the coupling. After that, the coupling can run freely on the shaft, disconnecting the traction motor from the cardan shaft.

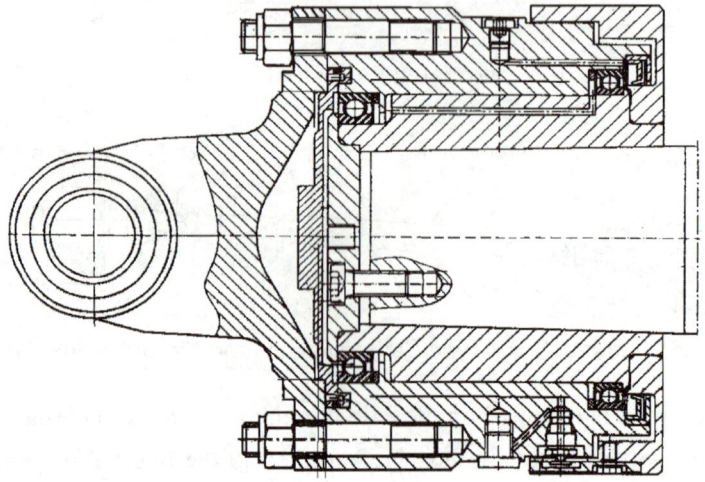

Fig.4.35　The Safeset Structure

cardan shaft transmission type carbody-mounted motor driving system mounts the traction motor on the chassis of the car body, which greatly reduces the unsprung mass and the inter-sprung mass compared with mounting the motor on the bogie frame. By minimizing the unsprung and unsprung mass, vibrations and shocks between the wheel and the track due to the rail are greatly reduced. In this way, the force on the bogie can be relatively reasonable, and the vertical and lateral action force between the wheel and rail can be reduced. The design of the cardan shaft transmission type carbody-mounted motor driving system structure makes each bogie only need one traction motor. The traction motor is easily accessible from the side and under the car body for servicing, and the traction motor can be easily removed without removing the bogie from the body. This design greatly improves the reliability and maintainability of the traction motor.

Cardan shaft transmission type carbody-mounted motor driving system has the following advantages:

(1) The traction motor is completely mounted on the car body, which can further reduce the mass of the bogie (especially the rotational inertia of the bogie), and improve the stability and stability of the bogie during high-speed operation.

(2) The space around the axle is released, which is conducive to the mount of other equipment (such as the foundation brake device).

(3) The working conditions of the traction motor are fully improved. Improve the reliability and maintainability of the traction motor.

(4) The unsprung mass of the primary suspension is small, and the wheel-rail action force is small.

(5) The traction motor can be easily removed without removing the bogie from the car body.

However, cardan shaft transmission type carbody-mounted motor driving system has high requirements on the manufacturing process of the cardan shaft, and the entire driving device has a complex structure and high manufacturing cost. In addition, because the entire motor bogie has only one power axle and the other axle is a non-power shaft, that is, each motor bogie is only equipped with one set of traction motor and driving device. On the one hand, the structure of the motor bogie is further simplified and meets the requirements of lightweight design, but on the other hand, the adhesion conditions between the driving wheelset and the rail are also deteriorated. In China's high-speed railway system. CRH5 EMUs use cardan shaft driven overall carbody-mounted motor.

Driving device of CRH3 EMUs:

The driving device of the CRH3 EMUs adopts WN coupling frame-mounted motor driving system. The traction motor is mounted onto a suspended motor frame, as shown in Fig.4.36. The motor frame is laterally elastically. A safety catch is provided to carry the traction motor and to avoid vertical movements down to the track. The safety catch projects into a bracket at the bogie frames' centre transverse and the motor frame. A WN coupling is provided between traction motor and gear unit in order to allow for vertical movements of the gear unit. The main technical parameters of the driving device of the CRH3 EMUs are shown in Tab.4.2.

Fig.4.36 The Traction Motor of CHR3 EMUs

Tab.4.2 The Main Technical Parameters of the CRH3 EMUs Driving Device

Driving device technical parameters	
Rated power	560 kW
Rated speed	4100 r/min
Rated torque	1200 N · m
Maximum speed	5891 r/min
Maximum starting torque	3100 N · m
Gear Ratio	2.793
Traction motor weight	750 kg
Gearbox weight	295 kg
Ventilation method	Forced ventilation

4.2.7 Foundation Brake Device

The braking system is the most important system to ensure the safe operation of EMUs, and it is also a very complex system. When the EMUs brakes, the EMUs usually first uses regenerative braking to slow down the EMUs. When the regenerative braking force of the EMUs is insufficient, the air brake is combined to further decelerate or stop the EMUs.

The braking control system used by the EMUs is actually complementary and closely integrated with its traction drive control system. The traction system and the regenerative braking system belong to the same system, and they both take the traction motor as the control object. It's just that when the EMUs is operating, the motor works in the traction condition, and when the EMUs is braked, the motor works in the generator condition.

A complete braking system mainly includes two parts: the braking control system and the braking execution system. The brake control system is composed of the brake signal generation and transmission device and the brake control device, and the brake execution system is usually called the foundation brake device. Since the brake control system is no longer part of the bogie category, this book only discusses the foundation brake device.

The maximum deceleration of the EMUs is $0.8 - 1.0$ m/s^2. The emergency braking distance specified by the EMUs can be divided into: when the initial braking speed is 200 km/h, the emergency braking distance is less than 2000 m; when the initial braking speed is 160 km/h, the emergency braking distance is $\leqslant 1400$ m. In order to meet the above requirements or regulations, it is necessary to rely on a flexible, safe and reliable foundation brake device.

The foundation brake device is the final actuator of the EMUs braking system, and its main tasks are:

(1) Transfer the piston force generated by each brake cylinder to each brake shoe (or brake pad);

(2) Increase the piston force several times;

(3) Ensure that the pressure of each brake shoe (or brake pad) is basically equal.

The foundation brake device is a very important part in the bogie. It has many forms. According to the braking method, it can be divided into: tread shoe brake device, disc brake device (axle-disc brake and wheel-disc brake), magnet track brake, and eddy current brake.

1. Tread shoe brake device

Tread shoe brake is one of the most commonly used braking methods, and traditional locomotives and rolling stocks adopt this braking method. Since the EMUs needs to install a large number of electric traction and other equipment under the chassis of each car, the installation space for the foundation brake device is relatively limited. Therefore, the improved tread shoe brake method (unit brake) is often used on general EMUs, especially urban rail vehicles, as shown in Fig.4.37. It is composed of a brake cylinder, an automatic slack adjuster (It is used to adjust the clearance between the wheel and the brake shoe to keep the stroke of the brake cylinder piston within the set range, thereby preventing the attenuation of the braking force), etc., which saves a series of transmission components in the traditional basic brake device, thus greatly improving the transmission efficiency.

Fig.4.37 Tread Shoe Unit Brake

The unit brake has compact structure, high braking efficiency and flexible function, and is easy to achieve with little or no maintenance. Moreover, because of its automatic slack adjuster, the brake shoe gap can always be kept within the specified range without manual adjustment, which saves labor.

During the braking process, most of the kinetic energy of the EMUs is converted into heat energy through the friction between the brake shoe and the wheel and the friction between the wheel and the rail, and then finally dissipated into the atmosphere through the brake shoe and the wheel. During the braking process of the brake shoe, the ability of kinetic energy to be converted into heat energy is large, but the ability of heat energy to dissipate in the atmosphere is relatively small. When the required braking power is large, there may be a phenomenon that the heat energy cannot be dissipated in time and accumulate on the brake shoe and wheel tread. In this way, the temperature of the brake shoe and the wheel will increase, and in severe cases, the brake shoe will melt (cast iron brake shoe) or the wheel tread will crack. Therefore, when the brake shoe is used for braking, the braking power must be limited.

In the friction pair of the brake shoe and the wheel, the material of the wheel cannot be changed arbitrarily because the wheel is mainly responsible for the running function of the EMUs. To improve the performance of brake shoe braking, only by changing the method of brake shoe material. The early brake shoe material was mainly cast iron. In order to improve friction performance and increase wear resistance, most EMUs now use composite brake shoe. However, the thermal conductivity of composite brake shoe is poor. Therefore, powder metallurgy brake shoes with good thermal conductivity and good friction performance and wear resistance are currently used.

2. Disc brake device

Disc brakes are the most commonly used braking methods for EMUs. According to the different mount positions of the brake disc, the disc brake is divided into the axle-disc brake and the wheel-disc brake. The axle-disc brake means that the brake disc is directly mounted on the axle, as shown in Fig.4.38. The wheel-disc brake means that the brake disc is mounted on both sides of the wheel, as shown in Fig.4.39. The disc brake generally adopts the axle-disc brake. Only when the mount of the brake disc is difficult due to the traction motor and other equipment in the middle of the wheelset, the wheel-disc brake can be used.

Fig.4.38　The Axle-disc Brake

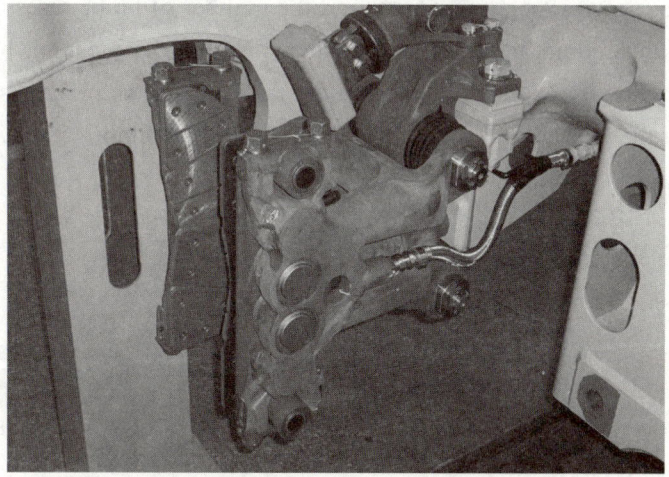

Fig.4.39　The Wheel-disc Brake

In order to simplify the structure, reduce the number of levers, reduce the weight, further improve the sensitivity and efficiency of the foundation brake device, reduce the failure rate and improve the reliability, the disc brake device usually adopts a modular design. That is, the brake cylinder, lever, brake caliper, automatic slack adjuster and brake pad holder are concentrated in one module to form a relatively independent brake unit. The mounting of the disc brake unit to the across beam or end beam of the bogie frame can be completed with only a few bolts.

The working principle of the disc brake: When braking, the brake pipe sends the pressure air into the brake cylinder to close the brake caliper, which in turn drives the brake pad to clamp the brake disc, and friction occurs between the brake pad and the brake disc, hindering wheelset rotation. Finally, through the adhesion between the wheel and the rail, a force opposite to the movement direction of the wheelset is generated to decelerate or stop the wheelset. When released, the pressurized air in the brake cylinder is discharged, and the rods drive the brake pads away from the brake disc.

During the braking process, most of the kinetic energy of the EMUs is converted into heat energy through the friction between the brake pads and the brake disc, the friction between the wheels and the rail, and finally dissipated into the atmosphere.

Disc brakes are easier to obtain much greater braking power than shoe brakes. Brake discs are made of cast iron, cast steel and forged steel, and brake pads are also made of synthetic materials, powder metallurgy and other materials. Due to the low speed of urban rail vehicles, cast iron discs are generally used to form brake pads. For the selection of the material composition of the synthetic brake pad, in addition to meeting the requirements of braking friction performance, the impact on environmental pollution must be considered, and it should meet the relevant environmental protection requirements. For high-speed EMUs, the design speed is relatively high, and the number of brake discs can be increased to meet the braking requirements. If the number of brake discs cannot be increased, the braking requirements can be met by changing the materials of the brake discs and pads (for example, powder metallurgy brake pads are selected, as shown in Fig.4.40).

Fig.4.40　Powder Metallurgy Brake Pad

Disc brakes are the foundation brakes commonly used by almost all EMUs, mainly due to:

(1) The disc brake device replaces the friction of the brake shoe on the wheel tread, so there is no thermal influence on the wheel. Moreover, the wear of the wheel is also reduced, and the service life of the wheel is prolonged.

(2) The heat dissipation performance of the disc brake is better, the friction coefficient is stable, and a relatively constant braking force can be obtained. Also, its thermal capacity allows it to have high braking power.

(3) The material of the brake disc and pad can be freely selected, so that the friction pair has the best braking parameters, and a higher and stable friction coefficient can be obtained. Therefore, the pressure of the brake pad can be reduced, the size of the brake cylinder and the lever can be reduced, and the weight of the brake device can be reduced.

(4) Disc brakes are economical to use. Generally speaking, the pad area of disc brake is larger than that of shoe brake, the compressive stress is smaller, and the wear rate is smaller.

(5) After the disc brake replaces the tread brake shoe, the unsprung weight will be increased, and the adhesion coefficient between the wheel and rail will be reduced.

3. Magnet Track Brake

Magnet track brake is a kind of non-adhesive braking that makes the train decelerate or stop by the adsorption between the electromagnet installed under the bogie and the rail.

The principle of magnet track brake is shown in Fig.4.41. A braking electromagnet is mounted between the two wheels on the same side under the side frame of the bogie. When braking, put down the electromagnet and excite the excitation coil on the electromagnet at the same time to generate a strong magnetic field, so that the wear plate of the electromagnet is adsorbed on the rail. The braking force is generated by the sliding friction between the wear plate on the electromagnet and the rail, which converts the kinetic energy of the train into heat energy and dissipates it in the atmosphere. Relieving braking the current in the excitation coil is cut off to remove the magnetic field, and the electromagnet is retracted away from the rail.

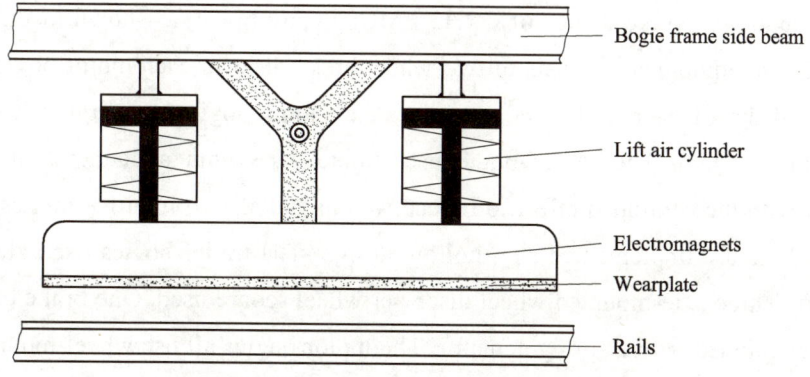

Fig.4.41　Magnet Track Brake Structure

Magnet track brake can obtain greater braking force, and is often used as an effective supplementary braking method for emergency braking of high-speed EMUs and light rail vehicles.

4. Eddy Current Brake

Eddy current brake is a non-contact electromagnetic braking method.

It uses the conductor (ECB disk) to cut the magnetic field lines in the magnetic field to generate eddy current, which makes the conductor (ECB disk) heat up, consumes the energy of train motion, and achieves the purpose of decelerating or stopping the train.

The working principle of eddy current braking is: when braking, the electromagnet is energized to generate a magnetic field. The ECB disc mounted on the axle rotates in the magnetic field to cut the magnetic field lines. The interaction between the ECB disc and the magnetic field will hinder the rotation of the wheelset. Finally, the adhesion between the wheel and the rail generates a force opposite to the movement direction of the wheelset, making the wheelset Slow down or stop. This electro-magnetic-thermal interaction between the ECB disc and the magnetic field is the source of the braking force. When the brake is released, the electromagnet is powered off, and the magnetic field disappears. Although the ECB disc still rotates in the magnetic field, there is no magnetic field obstruction.

Eddy current braking is non-contact, the braking electromagnet and ECB disc do not come into contact at any time, so there is no friction and of course wear is avoided. Since the ECB disc and the braking electromagnet do not come into contact during the braking process, the wheel and the frame will never be rigidly connected during this process, which will greatly reduce the instantaneous force between the wheel and rail and reduce wheel and rail damage.

Foundation Brake Device of CRH3 EMUs:

The foundation brake device of CRH3 EMUs is disc brake, as shown in Fig.4.42 and Fig.4.43. Brake equipment consists of two wheel brake disks at each motor bogie axle and axle brake disks of each trailer bogie axle. The motor bogie uses brake discs with a diameter of 750 mm. The trailer bogie uses brake discs with a diameter of 640 mm. Consistent with the continued effort to reduce weight and also to improve the testability of the axles, these are implemented as a hollow design. The trailer bogies use axle-mounted brake disks. Three axle-mounted wheel discs per wheel set are used. One brake caliper unit per axle is equipped with a spring actuator. The motor bogies all use wheel-mounted brake disks. Each wheel is equipped with a wheel mounted brake disc.

Fig.4.42   The Axle-disc Brake of CRH3 Motor Bogie Axle

Fig.4.43   The Wheel-disc Brake of CRH3 Trailer Bogie Axle

4.3   Maintenance of EMUs Bogie

In the level I maintenance of the CRH3 EMUs, the maintenance of the bogie part was completed by two staff members. The maintenance process of the bogie can be divided into maintenance when the EMUs is powered off and maintenance when the EMUs is powered on. The main maintenance tools used are: helmet, flashlight, walkie-talkie, steel ruler, cotton cloth, feeler gauge, ratchet wrench, and four corner keys. It should be noted that after the EMUs enters the maintenance shed the brake disc and brake pad may still be in a high temperature state, so do not touch it directly with your hands.

After the EMUs stopped in the maintenance shed, the staff applied for the power-off operation. After confirming that the EMUs was powered off and the relevant safety prevention and control devices were in place, the maintenance items for the bogie are shown in Tab.4.3.

Tab.4.3 Bogie Maintenance Guide

No.	Maintenance item	Maintenance guide	
1	bogie rail guard	① There is no obvious mechanical damage to the bogie rail guard device, all parts are complete, and the installation is firm and not loose. ② The bolts of all parts are securely attached, and the anti-loosening markings are not misaligned. ③ The height of the bogie rail guard device from the rail surface meets the limit regulations	Rail guard
2	Sanding device	① There is no obvious mechanical damage to the sanding device and the parts are complete and the installation is firm and not loose. ② The sanding device is hoisted and installed firmly without loss. ③ The bolts of all parts are securely attached, and the anti-loosening markings are not misaligned. ④ The height of the nozzle of the sanding device from the rail surface meets the limit regulations	Sanding device
3	Motor wheel	① The limits of tread circumferential wear, local concave and scratch depth, rim thickness, tread peeling, rim rolling width, etc. shall not exceed the limit. ② The appearance of the wheelset axle box device is good, there is no obvious mechanical damage, and the parts are complete and not loose. ③ The crack of the roulette disc is within the safe range, and the length of the crack on the disc surface along the radial direction does not exceed the limit. The roulette bolts are installed firmly, and the anti-loosening marks are not misaligned	

Continue

No.	Maintenance item	Maintenance guide	
3	Motor wheel	④ The surface of the anti-corrosion coating of the axle body is not damaged and peeled off. ⑤ The thickness of the friction ring of the brake disc, surface scratches, concave wear, and inclined wear meet the limit requirements. ⑥ Brake caliper and brake disc inspection: • The appearance of the brake pad holder is in good condition and the installation is firm. • The thickness of the brake pads does not exceed the limit, and the brake pads are not installed in reverse; • The brake caliper device has complete accessories and is in good condition; the suspension parts are complete and free of cracks, the mounting bolts are tightened without loosening, and the anti-loosening marks are not misaligned. • The surface cracks and thickness of the brake disc friction plate are within the limit, the bolts are installed firmly, and the anti-loosening marks are not misaligned. • The gap between the brake disc and the brake pad meets the limit requirements	Brake calipers
4	Motor power connector	① The power cables are not damaged and fixed well. ② The bolts are installed firmly, and the anti-loosening marks are not misaligned	Motor power connector
5	Gearbox and bracket	① The oil level of the gearbox is within the normal scale range. Suspension accessories are complete and the installation is firm.	Gearbox

Continue

No.	Maintenance item	Maintenance guide	
5	Gearbox and bracket	② The gearbox speed sensor, oil filling hole cover, oil drain hole cover, etc. are installed tightly, and the anti-loosening wire is in good condition without loosening. ③ The gearbox is securely hoisted and installed securely without deformation. ④ There is no oil leakage outside the gearbox. ⑤ All parts of the gear box bracket are complete, and there is no obvious mechanical damage or loosening. ⑥ The bolts connecting the gearbox bracket and the gearbox are firmly installed, and the anti-loosening marks are not misaligned. ⑦ The rubber spring has no cracks	Bracket Gearbox oil level	
6	Coupling	① There is no obvious mechanical damage to each part of the coupling, the accessories are complete, and the installation is firm. ② The bolts are installed firmly, and the anti-loosening marks are not misaligned	Coupling	
7	Traction motor	① The components of the traction motor have no obvious mechanical damage and signs of being hit, and the components are complete and firmly installed. ② The motor damper has no obvious mechanical damage, and the installation is firm and there is no oil leakage		
		Traction motor	Motor damper

Continue

No.	Maintenance item	Maintenance guide
8	Traction motor hanger	① The parts of the motor hanger have no obvious mechanical damage, the accessories are complete, and the installation is firm and not loose. ② The safety pin of the hanger is not damaged and the installation is firm. ③ The bolts are installed firmly, and the anti-loosening marks are not misaligned Motor hanger / Safety pin of the hanger
9	Brake cylinder	① The appearance of the brake air cylinder and the connecting device is good, there is no obvious mechanical damage, and the parts are complete and not loose. The rubber dust cover is undamaged. ② The brake air cylinder and each bolt of the connecting device are installed firmly, and the anti-loosening mark is not misaligned. Brake cylinder
10	Lateral damper	① The appearance of the lateral damper is good, there is no oil leakage, and the installation is firm and not loose. ② The damper seat has no cracks, the rubber stopper is not damaged, the bolts are installed firmly, and the anti-loosening marks are not misaligned Lateral damper

Continue

No.	Maintenance item	Maintenance guide	
11	Height control valve	The height control valve is firmly installed, the adjustment rod is not deformed, and the accessories are not missing	Height control valve
12	Lateral stop	① All components of the lateral stop device are complete, without obvious mechanical damage, and the installation is not loose. ② The sum of the distance between the traction center pin and the left and right of the lateral stop meets the regulations	Lateral stop
13	Center pin	① There is no mechanical damage to each part of the center pin, and the installation and fixation are good. ② The bolts of each part are installed firmly, and the anti-loosening marks are not misaligned	Center pin
14	Traction rod	① There is no crack or deformation in the traction rod and connecting rod device. ② The pressure plate and screw connection parts are complete, without cracks and deformation. ③ The bolts of all parts are installed firmly, and the anti-loosening marks are not misaligned	Traction rod

Continue

No.	Maintenance item	Maintenance guide	
15	Trailer wheel	① The limits of tread circumferential wear, local concave and scratch depth, rim thickness, tread peeling, rim rolling width, etc. shall not exceed the limit. ② The appearance of the wheelset axle box device is good, there is no obvious mechanical damage, and the parts are complete and not loose. ③ The surface of the anti-corrosion coating of the axle body is not damaged and peeled off. ④ The thickness of the friction ring of the brake disc, surface scratches, concave wear, and inclined wear meet the limit requirements. ⑤ Brake caliper and brake disc inspection: • The appearance of the brake pad holder is in good condition and the installation is firm. • The thickness of the brake pads does not exceed the limit, and the brake pads are not installed in reverse. • The brake caliper device has complete accessories and is in good condition; the suspension parts are complete and free of cracks, the mounting bolts are tightened without loosening, and the anti-loosening marks are not misaligned. • The surface cracks and thickness of the brake disc friction plate are within the limit, the bolts are installed firmly, and the anti-loosening marks are not misaligned. • The gap between the brake disc and the brake pad meets the limit requirements	Trailer wheel
16	Parking brake device	① All parts of the parking brake device have no mechanical damage and are well fixed. ② The bolts are installed firmly, and the anti-loosening marks are not misaligned Parking brake device	

123

When the power-off maintenance of the EMUs is completed, the staff must confirm that there are no operators under the car body and on the roof. After confirming that the power supply safety conditions are met, go through the catenary power supply procedures, and raise the pantograph of the EMUs. When the EMUs is powered on, the maintenance of the bogie in the level I maintenance is mainly to maintenance the parts on both sides of the bogie and the specific maintenance items are shown in Tab.4.4.

Tab.4.4

No.	Maintenance item	Maintenance guide
1	Axle box guidance of motor car	① The axle box hydraulic damper has no oil leakage, and the appearance is in good condition, the damper seat has no cracks. ② The axle box spring is not broken. ③ The appearance of the axle box is in good condition, and the bolt anti-loosening mark is not misaligned. ④ The sensor is installed firmly, and the wiring is not loose or damaged. ⑤ The appearance of the axle box guidance device is in good condition, and the mounting bolts are not loose Axle box guidance of motor car
2	Motor car bogie frame	① The bogie frame has no cracks. ② Each mounting seat on the bogie has a good appearance and no damage. ③ There is no damage to the emergency lateral stop, and the installation is in good condition. ④ The nameplates of the bogie are securely installed Motor car bogie frame

Continue

No.	Maintenance item	Maintenance guide	
3	Anti-roll torsion bar	① The torsion bar and connecting rod are installed firmly without cracks and deformation. ② The appearance of the joint bearing is in good condition. ③ The bolts of all parts are installed firmly, and the anti-loosening marks are not misaligned	Anti-roll torsion bar
4	Air spring	① The appearance of the air spring is in good condition and there is no air leakage. ② The mounting bolts of the bolster are firmly installed, and the anti-loosening marks are not misaligned	Air spring
5	Yaw dampers	① The yaw damper has no oil leakage and is in good appearance. ② The installation of the yaw damper is not loose, and the anti-loose mark is not misaligned, the damper seat has no cracks	Yaw dampers
6	Motor junction box	① The appearance of the motor junction box is in good condition and there is no damage. ② The motor junction box is well tightened, the bolts of each part are not loose, and the anti-loosening marks are not misaligned. ③ Each electrical connection line is intact and free of damage	Motor junction box

125

Continue

No.	Maintenance item	Maintenance guide	
7	Axle box guidance of trailer	① The axle box hydraulic damper has no oil leakage, and the appearance is in good condition, damper seat has no cracks, the installation bolts are fastened, and the anti-loosening mark is not misaligned. ② The appearance of the axle box spring is in good condition. ③ The appearance of the axle box is in good condition, and the bolt anti-loosening mark is not misaligned. ④ Each sensor is installed firmly, and the wiring is not loose or damaged. ⑤ The appearance of the axle box guidance device is in good condition, and the mounting bolts are not loose	Axle box guidance of trailer
8	Parking brake release handle	The appearance of the handle is in good condition, and all parts are firmly installed	Parking brake release handle

Homework

1. What are the components of the EMUs bogie?
2. What are the types of EMUs bogie frames?
3. How to distinguish between motor bogies and trailer bogies?
4. What is the difference between wheel-disc brakes and axle-disc brakes?
5. What are the components of axle box guidance?
6. Briefly describe the maintenance content of the EMUs bogie.

Chapter 5

EMUs End Connection Device Structure and Maintenance

Learning objectives

- Know the EMUs end connection device structure.
- Know the classification of coupler.
- Understand the action principle of EMUs coupler.
- Familiar with automatic coupler maintenance.

5.1 EMUs End Connection Device Structure

The end connection device ensures the mechanical connection, electrical connection and gas connection between vehicles. Moreover, the transmission of force between vehicles and the influence of EMUs gauge, aerodynamics and vehicle dynamics are solved. The end connection device is mainly composed of front assembly, couplers (automatic coupler, emergency adapter coupler, semi-permanent coupler), gangways, end connecting pipeline.

5.1.1 Front Assembly

The front assembly is composed of a front hatch and a hatch opening and closing mechanism. The hatch opening and closing mechanism can automatically and manually open the front hatch. Moreover, the front assembly has the functions of automatic and manual locking and unlocking of the front hatch, which is convenient for the reconnection of the EMUs and the coupling of the coupler during EMUs rescue. The structure is shown in Fig.5.1.

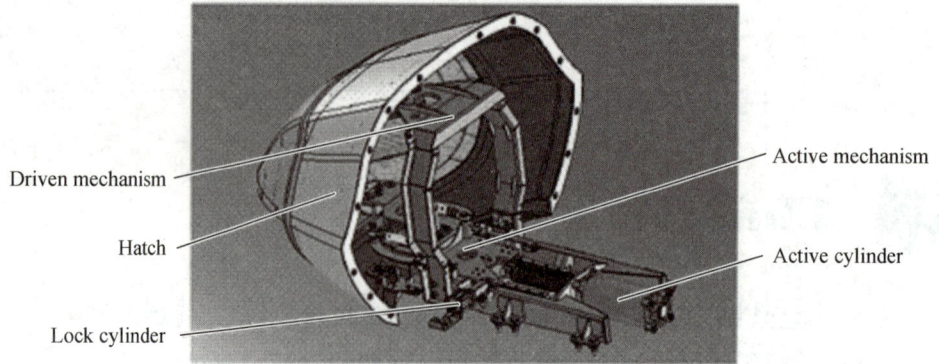

Fig.5.1　The Structure of Front Assembly

In the condition of reconnection, return and rescue of the EMUs, the opening and closing mechanism can be opened, and the automatic coupler can be extended to realize the connection of the vehicle. The EMUs uses an "energy-absorbing sandwich" structure on the front assembly of the head car, which absorbs energy in the process of being crushed during a collision, reducing damage to passengers.

5.1.2　Automatic Couplers

The automatic coupler allows the automatic coupling for regular shunting operations. During a mechanical coupling procedure with a vehicle of the same type, all electrical connections and pneumatic connections are automatically established. The front module of each end car is equipped with an automatic coupler. The automatic coupler is composed of coupler head, air pipe connection, coupler shank, earthing and other parts. The structure is shown in Fig.5.2.

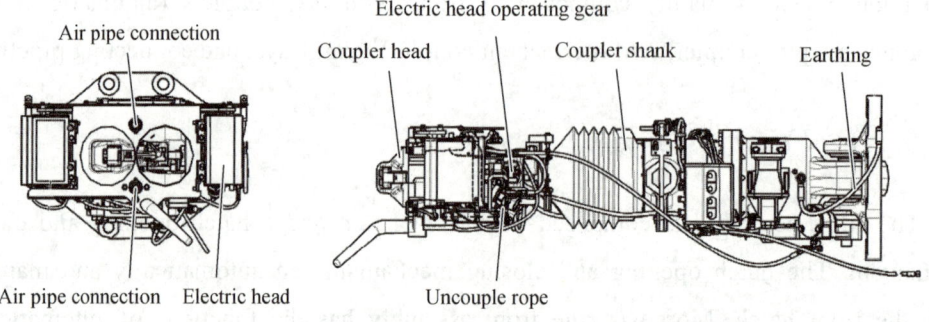

Fig.5.2　The Structure of Automatic Couplers

The coupling or decoupling of the automatic coupler can either be remotely operated by the driver in the cab or manually beside the track. In the event of an emergency (such as a failure or malfunction of the pneumatic system), the automatic coupler can be manually operated with or without compressed air. Surface of the coupler head of the automatic coupler is provided with a male cone and female cone, which allows automatic alignment and concentricity between the two couplers, and provides a large connecting range in the horizontal and vertical directions. When carrying out the rescue connection on the horizontal curve section, pay attention to manual assisted alignment in the horizontal direction. During the connection process, the internal connection mechanism rotates to connect the two hooks. At this time, the connection mechanism forms a complete parallelogram structure coupler.

5.1.3 Semi-Permanent Coupler

The semipermanent coupler is designed to ensure a permanent connection of railway vehicles which in traffic form a unit and therefore need not be separated unless in an emergency or in the workshop for maintenance. The coupler halves are connected by means of easily detachable muff couplings thus ensuring a rigid, slack-free and safe connection. The coupler permits coupled trains to negotiate vertical and horizontal curves and allows rotational movements.

Compared with the automatic coupler, the semi-automatic coupler removes the part of the electric head connection. Therefore, the extension and retraction of the semi-automatic coupler requires manual operation, but the mechanical connection can still be completed automatically. The structure of semi-permanent coupler is shown in Fig.5.3.

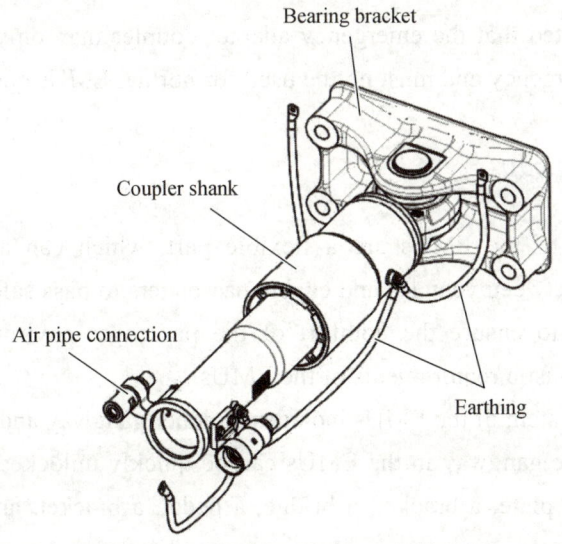

Fig.5.3 The Structure of Semi-Permanent Coupler

The semi-automatic coupler can be directly connected with the EMUs, or connected with the locomotive through the emergency adapter coupler.

5.1.4 Emergency Adapter Coupler

Each EMUs is equipped with an emergency adapter coupler, usually located in the middle car of the EMUs consisting out of several coupler parts.

The emergency adapter coupler is a component that connects with the locomotive when the EMUs needs to be rescued and returned by the locomotive. Structurally, one side of the emergency adapter coupler can be connected with the EMUs coupler, and the other side can be connected with the locomotive coupler, as shown in Fig.5.4.

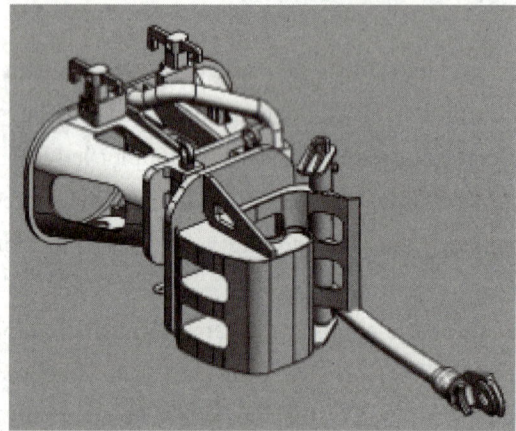

Fig.5.4 Emergency Adapter Coupler

It should be noted that the emergency adapter coupler may only be used for hauling trains in case of emergency and must not be used for normal EMUs operation.

5.1.5 Gangway

The gangways of the EMUs are a flexible part, which can absorb the maximum relative movement between vehicles and enable passengers to pass safely and conveniently. Moreover, in order to ensure the comfort of the passenger environment and meet the aerodynamic and acoustic requirements of the EMUs.

The gangway system of the EMUs includes an inner gangway and an outer gangway.

Both ends of the gangway in the EMUs can be quickly unlocked, and it consists of a bellows, a transition plate, a bracket, a bridge, a pedal, a bracket, and a leaf spring. The inner gangway can seal against noise, water, snow, and external air pressure, and has good heat insulation and sound insulation performance. The inner gangway's structure is shown in Fig.5.5.

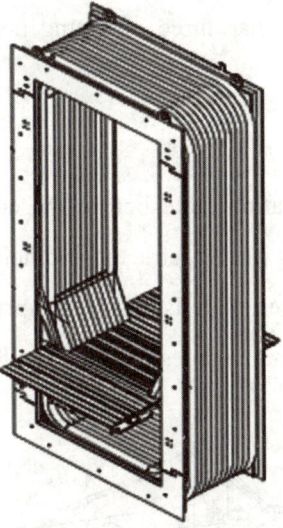

Fig.5.5 The Structure of Inner Gangway

The outer gangway is usually composed of rubber parts and aluminum alloy profiles, and its function is to reduce the running resistance of the EMUs and reduce the impact of airflow on the EMUs. The outer gangway does not affect the relative movement of the vehicle and does not produce abnormal noise or vibration. The outer gangway is shown in Fig.5.6.

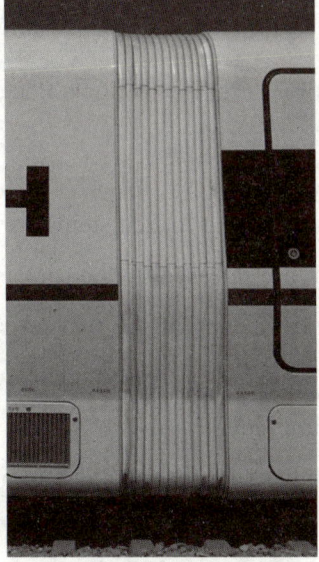

Fig.5.6 The Outer Gangway

5.2 Action Principle of EMUs Coupler

The coupler lock of EMUs has three operating positions: ready to couple, coupled position and Uncoupled position.

1. Ready to Couple

This position is the preparation state before the coupler is connected, as shown in Fig.5.7. At this time the coupling link is retracted and held by a ratchet and lies close to the edge of the male cone. The hooked plate is tensed by springs. The ratchet projects over the side of the coupler head casing and engages with the catch of the stem guide.

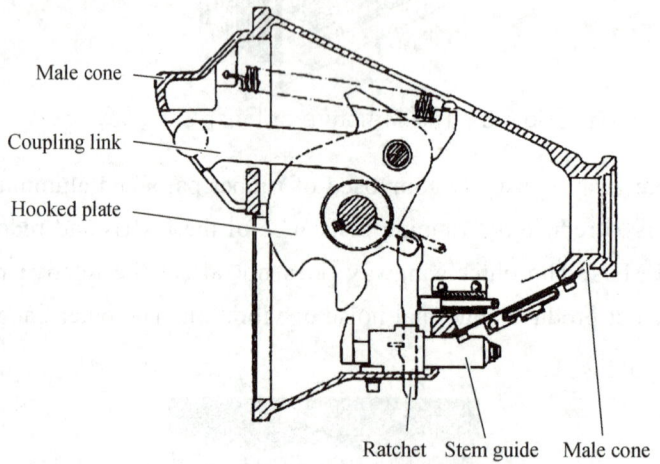

Fig.5.7 Ready to Couple Position

2. Coupled Position

as the coupler faces mate, the spring loaded stems are pressed backwards by the male cones against the ratchets which are released by the catches. By that the coupler locks are turned to the coupled position by means of the tension springs until the coupling links engage with the hooked plates which are pressed against a stop inside the coupler head casing. The coupled position is in Fig.5.8.

When coupled, the coupler locks form a parallelogram ensuring equilibrium of forces. In-voluntary unlocking is impossible. The coupler locks are subjected to tensile load only which is uniformly distributed onto both coupling links.

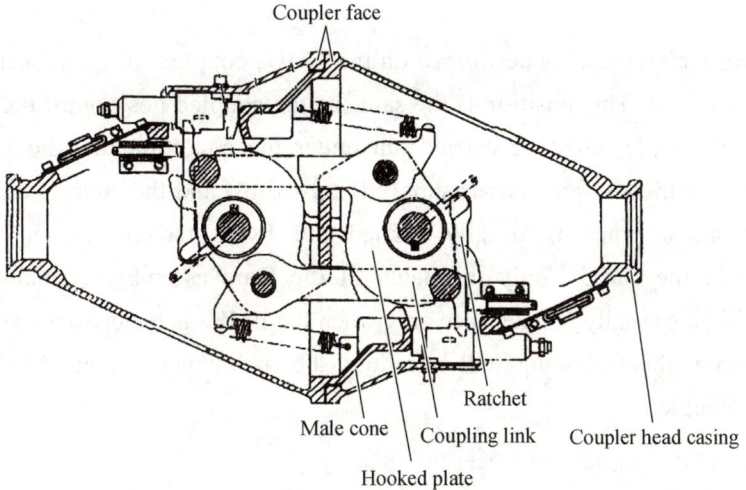

Fig.5.8　Coupled Position

3. Uncoupled Position

When uncoupling, the spring loaded hooked plates are turned until the coupling links are released from the hooked plates. The position of the coupler lock is retained as the ratchet has engaged with the stem. As the cars move apart, the spring loaded stem and the catch move forward and releases the ratchet. The coupler lock is turned by the action of the tension springs until the ratchet engages with the catch of the stem. The coupler lock is again ready to couple. The uncoupled position is in Fig.5.9.

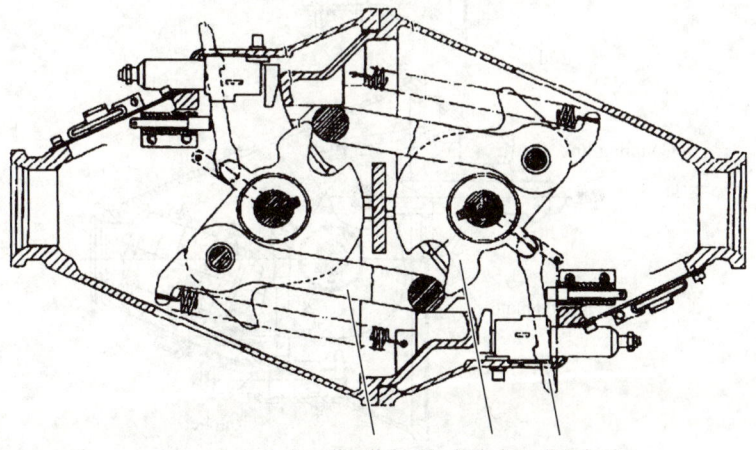

Fig.5.9　Uncoupled Position

5.3 EMUs Coupler Maintenance

Whenever maintenance is performed on the EMUs coupler, the coupler must be in the maintenance position. This position is the same as the coupled position of the coupler. The maintenance of coupler shall be carried out under the condition that the EMUs has no power supply and the compressed air supply is turned off and the coupler duct is drained. The coupler maintenance is usually carried out by 2 technicians. In the level Ⅰ maintenance of the EMUs, only the hatch of the front assembly is maintenance. The coupler should be specially maintenance only when the EMUs is maintenance at Level Ⅱ and above. Therefore, the following will introduce the maintenance content of the level Ⅱ maintenance coupler.

1. Automatic Couplers Maintenance

(1) Coupler cleaning

Use a rubber hammer to place the coupler in the maintenance position and perform a preliminary cleaning of the coupler, as shown in Fig.5.10.

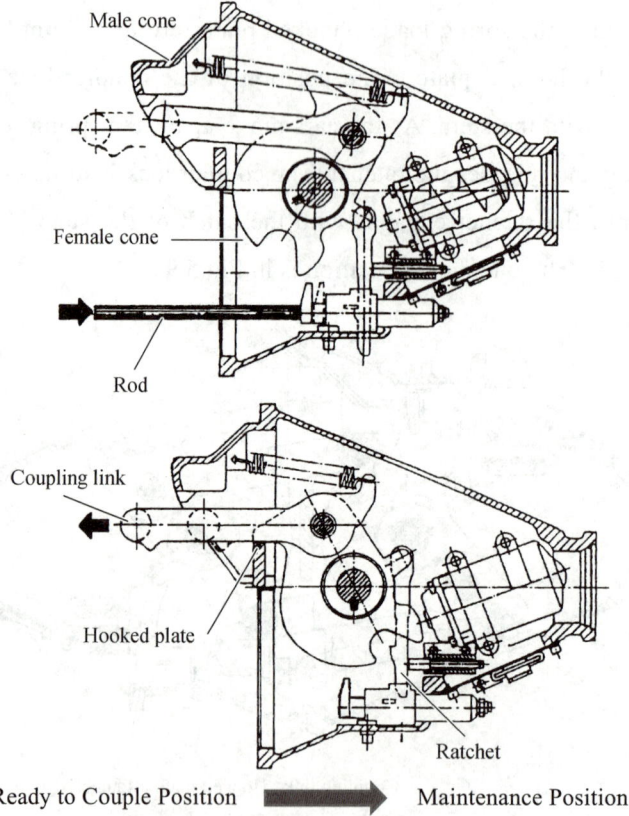

Fig.5.10　Place the Coupler in the Maintenance Position

When cleaning the coupler, in order to prevent the sprayed water mist from entering the electrical components of the coupler, it is necessary to select a suitable splash plate to cover the electrical components.

For large particles of dirt on the coupler, wipe with a dry cloth first, then a damp cloth. If the stains are stubborn, you can sprinkle detergent on the surface of the coupler, wait for the detergent to react for a certain period of time, and then wipe it off with a rag.

After the coupler has been cleaned, thoroughly inspect the coupler for obvious damage.

(2) Coupler Maintenance

The maintenance content of coupler components is shown in Tab.5.1.

Tab.5.1 Maintenance guide of coupler components

No.	Component	Maintenance guide	
1	Coupler head	① Check that the coupler lock is working properly. ② Lubricate the center pivot with a lube nozzle. ③ Lubricate the coupler lock with lubricating spray AUTOL TOP 2000. ④ Check the spring for damage and replace if necessary. ⑤ Reapply the anti-corrosion coating of coupler surfaces, male cone and female cone with ZINGA preservative	Lubrication nozzle on center pivot
2	Air pipe connection	Clean sleeve and gasket with a grease-free cloth	Gasket(A) and sleeve(B) Gasket and sleeve
3	Coupler shank	① Operate the telescopic device to extend and retract several times to check that it works smoothly. ② The locking device must automatically couple in either end position and uncouple upon activation	Coupler shank

Continue

No.	Component	Maintenance guide	
4	Bracket	① Clean bracket with compressed air or a dry rag and inspect for wear or damage and replace if necessary. ② Lubricate bare sliding surfaces with a thin layer of AUTOL TOP 2000	Bracket
5	Snap ring connector	Check for grease in the snap ring hole, re-grease if necessary	Snap ringconnector Snap ring connector

2. Semi-Permanent Coupler (Fig.5.11)

(1) Clean the coupler face, coupling link, remove the sundries. Apply Molik 1000 grease on the surface of the coupling link, and apply No. 2 extreme pressure lithium-based grease on the coupling surface. Pull the coupler unlocking handle to confirm that the coupler locking mechanism works well.

(2) Check that the coupler joint, joint buffer, bracket, support, support spring box, slide plate, and release handle are not bent, cracked, or damaged, and confirm that the installation state and connection state are not abnormal.

（3）Check the coupler, coupler support plate and buffer device to confirm that there is no crack or deformation in each part. All bolts are fastened without loosening, and the rubber parts are not aged, deformed or cracked.

Fig.5.11　Semi-Permanent Coupler

3. Emergency Adapter Coupler (Fig.5.12)

After initial cleaning of the emergency adapter coupler, visually inspect it for corrosion, wear and damage. Check the torsion spring for wear. If there is a problem, it needs to be replaced in time.

If the emergency adapter coupler is found to be loose during inspection, all fasteners such as screws, nuts, washers, retaining rings, helical rings and cylindrical pin must be completely replaced.

Fig.5.12　Emergency Adapter Coupler

Homework

1. What are the components of the EMUs end connection device?
2. What is the function of the emergency adapter coupler?
3. Briefly describe the working principle of automatic coupler?

参考文献

[1] 梁炜昭，黄孝亮，尚红霞. 动车组构造[M]. 北京：北京交通大学出版社，2017.

[2] 王连森，连苏宁. 动车组维护与检修[M]. 成都：西南交通大学出版社，2018.

[3] 中国国家铁路集团有限公司机辆部. 铁路动车组运用维修[M]. 北京：中国铁道出版社，2022.

[4] 王伯铭. 高速动车组总体及转向架[M]. 成都：西南交通大学出版社，2014.